M000309831

Today Everything Is Different

Today Everything Is Different

An Adventure in Prayer and Action

Dirk G. Lange

Fortress Press

Minneapolis

TODAY EVERYTHING IS DIFFERENT
An Adventure in Prayer and Action

Copyright © 2021 Fortress Press. Published by Fortress Press, an imprint of 1517 Media. All rights reserved. Except for brief quotations in critical articles or reviews, no part of this book may be reproduced in any manner without prior written permission from the publisher. Email copyright@1517.media or write to Permissions, Fortress Press, PO Box 1209, Minneapolis, MN 55440-1209.

Unless otherwise cited, the Scripture quotations are from New Revised Standard Version Bible, copyright © 1989 National Council of the Churches of Christ in the United States of America. Used by permission. All rights reserved worldwide.

Cover design: Alisha Lofgren
Cover image: Ai Nhan, Unsplash
Interior design and typesetting: PerfecType, Nashville, TN

Print ISBN: 978-1-5064-3347-9
eBook ISBN: 978-1-5064-3822-1

With deep affection for my parents

Ursula H. Lange
(1927–2020)

Gerhard Lange
(1924–1996)

Wir danken Dir, Herr, denn Du bist freundlich
und Deine Güte währet ewiglich.

We give thanks to you, God, for you are gracious
and your goodness endures forever.

Psalm 106:1

From "Thanksgiving at the End of the Meal"
—Martin Luther, *Small Catechism*

CONTENTS

ABBREVIATIONS

BC   *The Book of Concord: The Confessions of the Evangeli-cal Lutheran Church.* Edited by Robert Kolb and Timothy J. Wengert. Minneapolis: Fortress Press, 2000.

LW   *Luther's Works [American Edition].* 82 vols. planned. St. Louis: Concordia; Philadelphia and Minneapolis: Fortress, 1955–1986; 2009–.

WA   Luther, Martin, *Luthers Werke: Kritische Gesamtausgabe, [Schriften]* 73 vols. Weimar: H. Böhlau Nachfolger, 1883–2009.

WADB   Luther, Martin, *Luthers Werke: Kritische Gesamtausgabe, Bibel.* 12 vols. Weimar: H. Böhlau, 1930–1985.

INTRODUCTION

Prayer and Action: Leipzig, 1989

"Teach us to pray" (Luke 11:1). This short gospel request summarizes my own experience: all my life long I have been learning how to pray. I have had extraordinary teachers, none of whom knew in the moment that they were teaching me how to pray. Yet, they were teaching me how to live into and from the Lord's Prayer and how life can be shaped by the Psalms. This little book traces some of that teaching as I have experienced it and understood it. I hope to outline a theology of prayer that is rooted in Martin Luther's writing, particularly his Psalms commentaries, and that also intersects with a singular, historical event. Both a singular event (action) and a particular reflection (prayer) shape a theology, a word, an intuition about God.

This theological approach acknowledges God's word as something always latent within history, within every event, tracing its own way through and in the midst of all that most people understand history to be. Our history books have often focused on great personalities, on wars and conflicts and political intrigues. More recently, they have refocused attention to movements and forces that have been marginalized and written out of many history books, especially the history of women and the history of communities, such as African Americans, that were deemed insignificant to the dominant white and patriarchal story.

In his message for the World Day of Peace in 1996, Pope John Paul II writes that institutions of education "have a duty to lead children gradually to understand the nature and demands of peace within their world and culture. Children need to learn the *history of peace* and not simply the history of victory and defeat in war. Let us show them examples of peace and not just examples of violence!"[1]

In these pages, I will attempt to do that: provide an example of peace that silenced the powerful. This way of peace was discovered in communal prayer. It *was* communal prayer. No glittery programs or fancy methods or slick, innovative, online marketing was employed. Communal prayer was simply a place of encounter where people *saw* each other and shared their hopes and fears, their humanity. This encounter gave rise to something like a new language and an unexpected way forward. Today, everything is different.

> This way of peace was discovered in communal prayer.

The book is centered on the experience and witness of clandestine prayer groups in East Germany that, throughout the 1980s, continued to grow, becoming more public and occasioning massive demonstrations that finally resulted in the fall of the Berlin Wall (November 1989) and the collapse of communist

Europe. Even if initially underground, these prayer groups were an example of church engaged in the public space.[2] "The prayers held us together. Who prays, doesn't close their eyes, doesn't forget, or let things become unconscious," says Pastor Hans-Jürgen Sievers.[3] Prayer takes the faith community out into the street. These small groups of believers knew that God never ceased to engage the world, reclaiming and transforming it.

They also knew that God was not only in the midst of two or three who gathered to pray, but God was also in their neighbors, whether committed communists or atheists, no matter how they self-identified. Through prayer, a deep human reality was revealed—dare I call it a communion—that opened even the doors of their hidden spaces. The Holy Spirit prayed within them and awakened not only among them but within society the beautifully human desire for reconciliation, for peace, for justice. In the midst of the crowds demonstrating around the churches in the streets of Leipzig in 1989, people encountered something deeply human.[4]

"Lord, teach us to pray." The teaching didn't begin for me in my encounter with Christians and underground prayer groups behind the Iron Curtain, but this story begins with their witness. What I have only partially traced in these pages is not a precise reconstruction of what happened; rather, it is a reflection on how the Holy Spirit testified in and through these witnesses of faith, young and old, lay and ordained. Their own interpretation of the events is deeply rooted in a Lutheran understanding of baptismal vocation, as developed by Luther and further developed by Dietrich Bonhoeffer.

This book is a reflection on the tradition that shaped my family—the Lutheran confessing tradition. It is an attempt to describe something of a Lutheran spirituality, though it might be more accurate to say a baptismal spirituality. My encounter with many of these underground prayer groups was a lesson in the *Small Catechism*. Many of the young people in East Germany and their pastors were steeped in a deeply confessing tradition. They were committed to prayer—individual and communal— as a primary practice of baptism, embodying within their lives Luther's own commitment: "Nothing is so powerfully effective against the devil, the world, the flesh, and all evil thoughts as to occupy one's self with God's word, to speak about it and meditate upon it. . . . Indeed, this is the true holy water and sign that drives away the devil and puts him to flight."[5]

Many years later, I was able to visit with some of the Lutheran pastors and Catholic priests and young people (not so young anymore!) who were actively involved in the underground prayer groups during the 1970s and 1980s. They graciously gave me their time and shared, in retrospect, their reflections on the activity of the prayer groups throughout the 1980s. In the conversations, I was surprised that the word *resistance* (*Widerstand*) never surfaced. I asked about this and always received the same response. Pastor Sievers says it plainly: "Resistance wasn't a word that we used. We simply wanted a larger free space."[6] People gathered, prayers were held, a space was created, and doors were opened, simply as a way of living out one's baptismal vocation. They were fulfilling their baptismal vows. Through that practice and that faithfulness, the Holy Spirit worked something miraculous (*wunderliche*). Their faithfulness was a light that people saw, a light for which not they were glorified but their Father in heaven (Matt 5:16).

I do wish to acknowledge these witnesses. I am grateful to all those who spoke with me: Probst Heino Falcke, Pastor Christoph Wonneberger, Pastor Hans-Jürgen Sievers, Superintendent Frederich Magirius, Superintendent Martin Henker, Bishop Werner Leich, and Pastor Wolfgang Groeger.

I wish to thank Pastor Groeger and his spouse, Cornelia Groeger, in particular. They welcomed me generously. Pastor Groeger explored and shared with me his own insightful reflections on those times. He shared with me his pastoral heart, seeking to find a way in what was often a situation of hopelessness. I was struck that his own guides had also been Luther's guides. What does the first commandment mean by "You shall have no other gods"? The way of faith springs forth from this first commandment. And then also Psalms 1 and 85: truth and mercy shall embrace. You, the reader, will see how Pastor Groeger's witness has shaped my own theological narrative in this book.

Small Catechism: Shaping Faith

There is yet another, earlier teacher of prayer in my life.

Every day, before and after meals, my mother prayed. As I grew older and started confirmation at St. Stephen's Lutheran Church with Pastor Johan Kunkel, I discovered that my mother had always been praying the *Small Catechism* with us. She had many other prayers too, especially German hymns, some by

Luther, though most were by Paul Gerhardt, Matthias Claudius, and Jochen Klepper. She recited these hymns, prayers, and poems until the day she died.

Prayer shaped my life as a child. Prayer shaped my faith, just as prayer had shaped my mother's life and faith. In this life, the journey of faith is between death and life. Our sleeping and our rising again in the morning are like practice for that final passage . . . the night brings its restlessness and worries, its anxious moments when our heart and mind cannot always control wandering thoughts; the day too confronts us with happenings that do not always go the way we want them to go and with people who are not always who we wish them to be. Every day we die little deaths but we are always raised up again, given new beginnings. The *Small Catechism* outlines this journey for us. Luther describes it as a lifelong spiritual baptism.

God has engaged this journey with us. God immerses Godself into our journey, dying and living with us, never abandoning us, never letting anything separate us from God's love. God cannot be closer to us on this journey through both joys and sorrows. God's unconditional promise is witnessed in God's birth in a manger, in God's complete embrace of the human condition. But the wood of the manger is also, as Luther notes, the wood of the cross. Christ's birth is a birth into death so that no matter what or how or when death confronts us—and I mean death in its multiple guises—we know that Jesus has already covered us, wrapped us all in swaddling clothes, and is continuously opening for us, in this life, glimpses of the marvelous things God is doing.

My mother's death was peaceful. But she had already died many deaths in her life, from fleeing her home in January 1945 to escape the advancing Soviet army, from working in a forced labor camp, from seeing her father taken away and only learning twenty years later that he had been executed, to fleeing a second time, as a displaced person, and establishing a new life in Canada. Her life was a going out and a coming in. She struggled to live it, sometimes well, sometimes with difficulty, but always in the deep hope that God was keeping her, watching over her, protecting her so that the sun would not strike by day, nor the moon by night.

The deep hope that lived within her came to expression in many ways and opened up to a light shining in a suffering world, to that child born in a manger, to the fullness of God in a broken body. For her, the glimpse of that light and promise always meant going out and being there for others, for the neighbor. The neighbor, for her, was always and in particular the refugee seeking a home. My mother's prayer was expressed in action.

Justification: A Spirituality

Though this book is not explicitly about justification by faith alone, it does propose that justification and prayer go hand in hand. Prayer, individual or communal, is a language and a way God draws us deeper into the mystery of God's justifying action. Prayer is made possible because of God's mercy (God's promise that God hears prayer). Prayer is a space in which we encounter God's immeasurable goodness—that is, a space where we encounter God's unconditional promise: justification. Faith, only faith, apprehends God's truth as God's mercy and God's mercy for all as reconciliation. Luther describes it in this way, commenting on Psalm 85, "But the fact that [God] has mercy is [God's] truth. And so, when [God] has mercy, [God] becomes true [that is, God keeps faith and promise], and when [God] keeps faith or remains true, [God] has mercy. And both are in Christ."[7]

In Luther's early sermon on prayer, he reflects on a person's worthiness to pray. "We pray after all because we are unworthy to pray."[8] We are brought to prayer because we do not have all the answers, because we have nothing to justify ourselves before God, so we can only abandon ourselves to God. This abandonment happens in prayer. In prayer, we taste God's mercy and truth, both in Christ. In prayer, all is stripped away that keeps us imprisoned within ourselves so that only faith remains and God alone is worshipped in fulfillment of the first commandment.

> **We are brought to prayer because we do not have all the answers.**

Perhaps we do not think of the Ten Commandments as a spiritual guide, and yet that is what Luther proposes. There are two tablets, so to speak, of the law—two imaginary stones or, more helpfully, two deeply connected relationships described in the Ten Commandments. The first relationship is with God. This relationship can be defined by faith; only faith justifies—that is, makes us whole. The second relationship is with the neighbor. The first commandment invites us into this relationship of total dependence, of abandonment of self and all those things to which the self so readily clings. You shall have no other gods.

The second commandment—you are not to misuse the name of your God—admonishes us not to disregard God's name. We are to call on it, Luther writes, day and night, "to praise God's name, to confess [God's] grace, to give all honor to [God] alone."[9] God invites us into prayer as the means by which we discover what that name—Mercy—means, and how God manifests God's self among us and how faith is shaping us.

The third commandment calls on us to hallow the day of rest. The Sabbath, for Luther, implies engaging God's word as the focus of life, "meditating upon and pondering God's benefits, and, in addition, chastising oneself and keeping the flesh subdued." Keeping Sabbath is the encounter with God's goodness and reveling in that goodness to the point where all that is within us that is contrary to Christ is subdued. In this way—which can be a way of struggle and suffering, because sin does not like to die—faith strengthens itself and "through that very calling on the name of God and praising [God], faith grows and comes into its own."[10] Faith is exercised in prayer.

Faith then goes out in action or, in Luther's words, it "goes out into works." Bonhoeffer, writing from prison, proposes: "All Christian thinking, talking, and organizing must be born anew, out of that prayer and action."[11] Reflecting on the events in Leipzig in 1989, Pastor Sievers remembered, "Martin Luther King Jr. said after church we go into the street and if we are arrested, we will sing. I thought, that is what we must do as pastors."[12] Faith goes out into the world, into the street, unannounced, clandestinely opening ways of encounter for the truly human, for reconciliation. All then becomes praise within us, praise for God alone.

1

Spirituality

Work of the Holy Spirit

The slightest movement of your hand, and a kaleidoscope will transfigure into new patterns and colors, much like spirituality in Western culture: depending on the angle you take, you'll see a new image, new contours, a different array of light. Every community of faith has its own movement of the hand, its own perspective. Metaphors for faith create varied configurations. Within my own confessional setting (Lutheran), a deep tension plays itself out whenever spirituality is brought into focus. Though the exact term *spirituality* may not appear in Luther's writing, the terms *spiritual* and *spiritually* occur over and over again. Luther defines the entire life of a believer as a spiritual baptism—that is, a life marked by what God does in and through baptism and what baptism signifies. Faith—the Holy Spirit's work within us—gives shape to a spirituality that is the subject of this little book.

For many, spirituality simply means something more than or other than the daily, routine rhythms of life, something beyond this life or deeper. Often it is simply, as Ernest Becker puts it, the "urge for more life, for exciting experience, for the development of the self-powers, for developing the uniqueness of the individual creature."[1] This tendency confronts me with a question: Is spirituality truly the Holy Spirit's work, or is it the work of human longing? Is spirituality focused on the striving of the human spirit to move beyond or above or deeper into a communion with the created world (in whatever way, shape, or form— as banal as coffee or chocolate, as natural as outdoor activity, or as extreme as drugs or sex or alcohol), or is it the work of the Holy Spirit shaping life for us?

Another tension or struggle, one that I feel myself in my own prayer, in my own life: I am simultaneously attracted to and troubled by the notion of spirituality. I want to engage a practice, but I admit that I can't always maintain it. Or, the practice eventually dries up, so to speak. Spirituality as my work is not particularly successful! Yet, I realize that my whole life, the choices I have made, the interactions I have had or am having, even with you, the reader—all of these experiences are profoundly inhabited by a question about God and what God is doing in my life. Somehow, these interactions, events, words, sights, and smells all are pushing me toward or deeper into a spirituality.

What, then, is meant by the word *spirituality*? The subject has, of course, known an incredible resurgence over the past few decades. You don't need me to tell you how many books there are on spirituality, and not just on Christian spirituality, but any type, particularly Eastern spirituality (or spiritualities). In seeking to answer what is meant by spirituality, here is one of the questions to be posed: What distinguishes Christian spirituality from other forms of spirituality? I can only answer that question from my own embedded situation: I am a Lutheran, from a long line of Lutherans who trace their faith commitment to a particular (Lutheran) understanding of how God interacts with the world. My mother and her family were members of the Confessing Church in Germany during the Nazi regime. As a teenager, I sat for hours listening to my grandmother talk about what it meant for them to find ways of living faith, of embodying faith in a society that eliminated any hint of resistance. What are the contours of faith that arise out of a situation of duress? And what does that mean for lives today, living in the seemingly safe and privileged enclave of the Western world?

This book will dive into these questions, exploring some avenues through Scripture, liturgy, and experience. Spirituality has become an extremely important aspect of Western religious culture. Yet, I'm already tired of the phrase, "I'm spiritual but not religious." Those who claim the spiritual as opposed to religious identity (including many Christians) often define spirituality as moving beyond the body and out toward the transcendental. Sometimes they define spirituality as longing for a communion with an immaterial reality or ultimate meaning found deep within things. (Platonism always loves to creep in through the back door.) When that happens, however, an unfortunate dichotomy is established between the sacred and the secular, between a realm of spirit and a realm of bodies, between the immaterial and the material, and between heaven and earth. And earth always loses. Yet, contact with the body cannot be avoided. In Christianity, the religious always points to a body: to the body of God and the neighbor. A focus on spiritual practices as embodiment inherently values the corporeal, the physical, the material, the earth, and not just as instruments toward an end. Christianity has a word that is of great help to us: incarnational. Incarnational means God, who takes on human form—that is, a body. The word becomes visible. The word is seen and touched. That is how much God values the earthly. The dichotomy between body and spirit is dissolved. Jesus is God. The body of Christ shapes spirituality, shapes practice, shapes experience, shapes bodies.

> In Christianity, the religious always points to a body: to the body of God and the neighbor.

One unique characteristic of a Christian spirituality, then, is an encounter with a person, with another body, with an other. Such an encounter expresses itself (perhaps first of all) in conversation, in dialogue. The implications of such an encounter are immense, and they will fill up the pages of this book. A radical shift in perspective is implied: Christian spiritual practice does not have as its goal a centering or inner balance or unity or even silence. It is not striving toward a goal or ultimate meaning. Religious and spiritual persons alike often speak about centering prayer, but I have never found that such centering or inner balance is the primary characteristic or goal of my spiritual practice, of prayer. Particular to the Christian practice of prayer is a meeting, an encounter and dialogue with another, with the risen Christ. Even in the most personal and private prayer, in the most intimate and individual prayer, I am never alone. In prayer, another is in conversation with me. Struggling with and rejoicing in another characterizes this prayer. Even when the exterior form of prayer may be drawn from a wealth of different practices (repetitive prayer, meditating in silence, and so forth), these practices are different because they are rooted in a word that is first addressed to me from outside me, from another, from Jesus in baptism. Christian practice—or a baptismal spirituality—is deeply relational.

This dialogue and this encounter are an expression of that mystery of communion, which is the church in God's plan. This communion, however, is not just about "Jesus and me." This communion pushes each one toward a recognition of the Risen One in the face of every other, every neighbor, familiar and unfamiliar. Perhaps this helps explain why words have been so important in the Christian tradition. Words are understood not only as a form of communication (a function they don't always fulfill well), but also as a form of communion, as an expression of something much deeper than simply the mental, verbal, cognitive. "And the Word became flesh and lived among us" (John 1:14). Words embody, maintain, memorialize, ritualize, and—through the Holy Spirit—enliven the relation with the Risen One in a vast communion.

This incarnational reality has a second component to it, a corollary characteristic of Christian spiritual practice. As incarnational, Christian spirituality is not denying or distancing oneself from experience, but moving ever deeper into creation; into the struggle and groaning of creation; into the messiness of a God born in a manger, announced by shepherds, adored by wise men, and washed in a river; fasting in a desert; journeying without a home; eating with sinners; dying and rising. In this sense, spirituality is not a filter to purify oneself as if this world and life had to be first cleansed of debris. Quite the contrary, Christian spirituality allows me to sit in the messiness of creation as Job sat down among the ashes. A better metaphor might be that of a garden: all experiences, good and bad, clouds and sun, rain and dry, come together to help me grow.

> Christian spirituality allows me to sit in the messiness of creation.

Precisely because Christian spirituality is not an escape from creation and life, because it places me in the heart of my existence, it necessarily involves me in a struggle, a struggle with my experiences, a struggle with people and events, a struggle with all of life's circumstances, both those I can and cannot control. Of course, not all of life is a struggle. There are many joyful moments. There are many fun and amusing moments, many projects and hopes and dreams. But deep down, there is always a question, an unease, a struggle with meaning: What does this all mean? Who am I with my desires and longings, my emptiness and my confusions? How do I relate to this world and to my neighbor? To whom am I neighbor? How are my heart, body, soul, and mind engaged in this world?

Spirituality and Desire

There is a type of popular spirituality that considers discernment a question about *me*. The focus of discernment is then on my desire for God: What is the shape, the strength, the thrust of a desire deep inside me for fulfillment, for God? This focus has a long-standing tradition in Christian spiritual writing. It begins with the assumption that every human being has desire and somehow that desire is also a god. It might even believe that all desires are expressions, sometimes hidden expressions, of this desire for God. It states: Everyone has a spirituality (in fact, all of creation, not just humans, has a spirituality) because everyone has a desire—for happiness, for fulfillment. Desire of course is rooted in dissatisfaction, in a lack of something. Life is understood to be only half full (at best) or half empty (at worst). The question for spiritual practice then becomes: How is my desire refined, clarified, even purified so that I can better discern God? How is my desire channeled so that it leads me to happiness and delight? There is a curious focus here on the individual, on the ego and what *I* need or want. Discernment becomes about my well-being.

I once had a conversation with Brother Roger of Taizé. We were walking, as we often did, along some paths around the Church of the Reconciliation at Taizé. It was a little rainy—a typical October day in the southern countryside of Burgundy, France. It was late afternoon. Because of the drizzle, we had stepped in that big, silent, dark church for a moment. As our eyes adjusted to the warm light that the colorful stained glass windows filtered in, Brother Roger began talking about our vocation. All of a sudden, he looked at me and bluntly asked,

"What are we seeking?" I was only a young brother at the time, just in formation, and the question unsettled me. *I certainly hope he knows what we are seeking,* I thought. Of course, the question was only rhetorical. Brother Roger continued his reflection: "Is it to be happy? No! We are simply seeking to follow Christ." There is something disturbing in that insight. It says that someone could follow Christ and yet not be happy in this life. Some would then ask: So why follow Christ? Or, in disappointment, others might respond: That wasn't what I bargained for! But you, I believe, can see what is happening here. Following Christ can become just another thing I do for my own fulfillment, a spirituality that helps me discern my own meaning. Perhaps it puts me in contact with good people; perhaps it gives me a momentary community; perhaps it even gives some structure to my life. All of these things are important, but if I pursue them because I seek fulfillment, I may be in for a big disappointment.

When Paul writes,

> For we know only in part, and we prophesy only in part; but when the complete comes, the partial will come to an end. When I was a child, I spoke like a child, I thought like a child, I reasoned like a child; when I became an adult, I put an end to childish ways. For now we see in a mirror, dimly, but then we will see face to face. Now I know only in part; then I will know fully, even as I have been fully known (1 Cor 13:9–12),

he is expressing a manner of living now, in the today that God has made. Today, I live in this promise: I am fully known, even if I only know partially. This partial knowing shapes my daily experience, my journey, my obedience, and it creates a wonderful, delightful space in which I know that God is taking me by the hand. Too quickly, though, I want to take hold of the goal—the complete, the fulfillment, the ultimate meaning—and leave the partial behind. For some reason, I believe I have a right to the whole thing immediately. I want to see my desire fulfilled. Bonhoeffer speaks about such a self-centered desire as living in an emotional community rather than a spiritual community.[2] All of those things—community, companionship, an ordered life, joy—are only real (or true, for Bonhoeffer) when they are given as a gift to those who have followed Christ, because they struggled with Christ in the messy reality of their lives. They were obedient in the provisional and partial, always trusting the promise.

My very desire for God can trick me. I think that it brings fulfillment when really it so often focuses my eyes back on myself and my need. The Augsburg Confession, in defining original sin, states, "This means that from birth they are full of evil lust and inclination and cannot by nature possess true fear of God and true faith in God." This evil lust or concupiscence is not only of the flesh; it is also an inclination of the human spirit. A spiritual concupiscence, an inordinate desire that mixes God into and with all my desires, leads me to equate self with God. My desire, then, even my desire for God, almost always points me to a god of my own making and not to the incarnate God. Then I hide my face from the incarnate God, because that God is not pleasing to look at (Isa 52). My desire for God—spiritual concupiscence—itself must meet the cross.

Isn't this the direction of the first commandment? "You shall have no other gods." Luther's explanation analyzes the human tendency to create gods. A god is that to which I look for all good, and in which I find refuge and comfort in all and every desire and need. "Therefore," Luther writes, "to have a god is nothing else than to trust and believe in that one with your whole heart. As I have often said, it is the trust and faith of the heart alone that make both God and an idol."[3] Wherever the heart places its trust, there is its god. Human beings like to create their own gods. They create gods in their own image, thereby making themselves the center of their own spirituality. Of course, I will always prefer the god I have created for myself, because that god will be much more accommodating of me.

This brief introduction to Christian spirituality leads to an unexpected place. Christian spirituality is not so much about finding an inner balance, a centeredness in life, an essential and pure desire, or a happiness or well-being. Christian spirituality, or baptismal spirituality, is about God inserting you and me, seekers all, into God's plan. This spiritual journey is a risky one. It means constantly starting anew. Today, every day, everything is different. That is the adventure of faith. Perhaps that is why you are reading this book, for you intuit that this journey, like Abraham's journey with Isaac, demands your whole being, on many levels of existence, some you have been unaware even exist. It demands a deep attentiveness to God's voice calling out in the most unexpected places and ways. Attentiveness or vigilance is an even better expression of that fundamental stance toward the

world around us. With vigilance comes patience and persever-
ance. This journey is about obedience.

Let's explore an example of obedience and vigilance, one
that opens like a modern-day Psalter with thanksgiving, lament,
and commitment. It's an example of baptismal spirituality in the
public space (if even initially very quietly). This story of liberation took place in the journey of clandestine prayer groups in
East Germany and their eventual overwhelming manifestation in
the fall of the Berlin Wall in 1989. These communal prayers
embodied in surprising ways this
return of the Christ event, the paschal event, in particularly life-giving
ways, not only for the individuals
involved but for an entire society.
The circumstance and conditions in
which it took place are too unique
to be transported into another context. This fact frees you and me

> This spiritual
> journey is a risky
> one. It means
> constantly
> starting anew.

from the desire to simply imitate it. In those clandestine prayers,
where the faith community struggled with and rejoiced in God's
word, where both fear and sweetness were experienced, I witnessed communities rooted in a simple prayer, trusting in the
Spirit obediently and innovatively, stubbornly and creatively. On
my own journey, I experienced both that struggle and that sweetness, if only partially, as I visited several of these underground
prayer groups in East Germany in the early 1980s. Via these
communities of faith, I learned what God can accomplish
through daily prayer in psalms and intercession.

A Liturgical Event

This story is about one specific, historical liturgical event. But first, I want to ask a pneumatological (Spirit-filled) question— not what that event *was*, but what the event *becomes*, and especially what it becomes today for the worship community and for me as part of it. How is it an example according to Scripture? My reason for this question is simple: If someone can speak about an event as if they know what happened, then they have confined that event to its place, they control it, and perhaps in that way they make sure it cannot challenge them. But I argue that there is something in every event that remains unknowable, something that cannot be represented, something that continually comes back, something unexpected.[4] The Spirit blows where it wills, continually opening new ways in new contexts. So perhaps I could also ask: What is it in this particular liturgical event—this prayer—that continually returns to question, to haunt, and to call out to me? How is this event a happening that reveals to me what a baptismal spirituality is all about and how the Holy Spirit acts?

This singular, historical, liturgical event occurred in Bonhoeffer's homeland just a little more than forty years after his death. The fact that it happened in the former East Germany is not incidental; it is significant. The church leaders who helped set the stage for this event were students of Bonhoeffer, and they were intensely concerned about witnessing Christ in a communist state (the former German Democratic Republic). They were pressed to define church in a religionless context. They wondered what it means to, as Bonhoeffer writes, "participate in the worldly tasks of life in the community, not dominating, but helping and serving." What does it mean to "tell people in every calling what a life with Christ is, what it means 'to be there for others'"?[5] They were continually asking themselves, Who is Christ for us today, and what does it mean for the way we live? One of their best theologians, Probst Heino Falcke, boldly defined the term for the church in a socialist state: church for others.

Many hopefully remember fall 1989 in Eastern Europe, particularly in East Germany, if only in the TV coverage of hundreds of thousands of people marching in the streets with lighted candles. The collapse of communist Europe had already begun earlier that year in Poland, but it took a visible form in East Germany. The entire order of a tightly controlled system was in disruption. Leipzig and Dresden were but two cities among many where this large manifestation occurred, bringing with it systemic upheaval. Some years later, as Ronald Reagan was being eulogized and again as Margaret Thatcher was being remembered, commentators and pundits alike stated that they were to be thanked for bringing down the Berlin Wall. Such interpretations that wish to glorify power (or, in the critical words of the psalmist in Ps 147:10, that rely on the strength of horses) belong to Western cultural mythology, more specifically to American mythology. Having worked in the underground church of the former East Germany and Czechoslovakia during the 1980s, I witnessed another reality that was far more significant in bringing down the wall. That the revolutions of 1989 are labeled peaceful revolutions is not without reason.

What was striking with the manifestations in Leipzig and other cities in fall 1989 was that they started in churches, with evening prayer. Throughout the 1980s (and in fact long before), there were many clandestine (and not-so-clandestine) groups meeting in apartments, occasionally in churches, or on weekend hiking or camping trips. These groups were small; sometimes only four or five people. They gathered for prayer, for discussion. They gathered to have a free space—*freiraum*—in which to be silent, to sing, and to hope. Some of these groups met in many different cities. They gathered for fellowship and were not meant to be political.[6] More official groups formed as well, notably in Dresden in November 1980, with the first gathering of the Ten Days for Peace (*Friedensdekade*). Subsequently, the groups organized regular prayers for peace. The free space that the church could provide in the heart of society was critical not only for its own life but for many others who did not identity as Christians. These free spaces gave an opportunity to various groups who were critical of the regime, groups that met for specific purposes, such as peace and environmental causes. They all found a home in the church. The groups were protected by the official church even if the Stasi (the secret police) regularly infiltrated them. Because of the possibility for free speech, even to discuss politics and economics, these gatherings began to attract non–church members as well.

The majority of these groups gathered for discussion and for what they often called public (though not always that public) communal prayer. The young people would pray for those who died in the fight against tyranny and those who were imprisoned; they would open the floor so that people could share their own alienation and exclusion; and they would remember the promise of the coming kingdom. God's word was at the heart of these prayers, a word that disrupted and reconfigured the cultural myths with which the participants lived. Often, at the end of prayers, they would light small vigil candles. The church has an ancient tradition of lighting candles as a sign of hope and communion. It stems from the celebration of the Easter Vigil, when, in the darkest part of the night, the paschal candle is lit, and then subsequently all other candles in the church and those held by the assembly. The community of Taizé, with its own practice of celebrating the paschal mystery every weekend of the year (with prayer around the cross on Friday and a mini Easter vigil on Saturday, culminating in the Sunday eucharistic celebration), popularized both this prayer around the cross and the lighting of the vigil candle. But the lighting of candles or a fire is also an ancient human tradition that predates Christianity and crosses religious boundaries. The symbol of light touches the depth of people's hearts. It is an ecumenical symbol, where *ecumenical* means the whole gathered household, all of humanity. It is

> The church has an ancient tradition of lighting candles as a sign of hope and communion.

also an interreligious symbol. Nonbelievers as well understood the candles; they didn't understand the prayers or the sermons, but the candles spoke to them.

With many ups and downs, these prayers slowly grew throughout the 1980s in number and size. At the same time, a more politically oriented prayer began to develop, known as the *Friedensgebete*—prayers for peace. This cycle of prayer was initiated and developed by the ecumenical youth movement in East Germany, along with the Evangelical Church in the German Democratic Republic. The ten days of prayer for peace were attached to the traditional Buss und Bettag (Day of Prayer and Repentance), which has deep roots in the tradition of Germany's Protestant churches as a special day of prayer in the midst of danger and need. In East Germany, this day was no longer a state holiday and therefore did not have much meaning for people or even for the congregation, but the youth saw it as an opportunity. This day received a new meaning, a new content, as a time of ardent prayer for peace. There was a prayer at midday on Buss und Bettag. The bells would ring at noon. They prayed with a common text for peace and invited people to pray along. This pattern became the structure for the ten days of prayer leading up to Buss und Bettag, except the time was transferred to the evening. For ten days at 6 p.m., people would pray, no matter where they found themselves.

The prayers became more and more difficult to control. They often were led by different groups with different themes. There wasn't much consistency among them. Someone attending never knew quite what to expect. Perhaps this is why they waned in the mid-1980s. Then the church authorities took things in their own hands, demanding a certain structure to the prayers. The superintendent in west Leipzig, Friedrich Magarius, asked one of the pastors, Christopher Wonneberger, to organize the prayers in the St. Nicholas Church (Nikolaikirche). He started by getting little groups, one by one, to lead the prayers there. Attention was to be paid to the liturgy, but equally important was the sharing of information within the time of prayer, information that people could not get in other places. All the pastors were also admonished: they were responsible for what happened in their parishes. Many other currents within East German society, and particularly life in the industrial (and very polluted) city of Leipzig, contributed to an ever-growing interest and participation in the prayers.

Pastors, such as Wonneberger, actively sought ways for the church to connect to the aspirations and movements in the street. Wonneberger opened his parish, which was in one of the most socially challenging and poorest neighborhoods of Leipzig, to artists. Authors could read their works there. Musicians censored by the state had a venue to perform. Protest songs were encouraged. Many highly gifted singers who never could perform in the St. Thomas Church (Thomaskirche) found a home there.[7] The church became a hub of cultural exchange, while at the same time tending to a life of prayer.

In summer 1989, when the church in East Germany held its Kirchentag,[8] a question arose: Can protesters take part? In response, Pastor Wonneberger organized a parallel Kirchentag called Stadtkirchentag (City/Church Days) to provide room for their voices. The wordplay *city/church* was fecund with significance. Finally, in summer and fall 1989, the prayers erupted into the streets, especially in Leipzig, in what came to be known as the Montagsdemonstrationen. The public communal prayer at the St. Nicholas Church in Leipzig was one of the main gathering places, though not the only one in Leipzig. In summer 1989, there already were seven thousand people attending, then twenty thousand, then seventy thousand, then three hundred thousand, then over half a million people. Of course, these numbers are like the numbers in Acts—difficult to estimate—but there were many, many people. Obviously, the church could not contain the worshippers, and they poured out into the streets with their candles in hand. They were like a liturgical procession moving with solemnity, not toward some high altar, some mythical center of meaning, but moving sometimes with song, sometimes silently, always with determination into the world.

Pastor Sievers notes: "I preached following Martin Luther King Jr. Just as in Birmingham, they walked and walked and became adults, no more like children. Now, I preached, we are walking."[9]

The openness of this communal prayer, taking the risk of walking in the street, brought many other people into the street. The common prayer listened to and met the aspiration from the street. The prayers went out like disciples into the darkness of their world. They went out with their own fear, their own anxiety and darkness, for they did not know what would greet them in the streets. Many were remembering Tiananmen Square, China, from earlier that year; but they went out with prayer and in a living hope. They went out with their candles lit. The candle became a gospel paradigm, not a religious paradigm. Through this communal adventure in prayer, the young people rediscovered a paradigm that was something like a *Via Lucis*, a way of light.

The metaphor of light—light in the darkness, light as hope, light as way—became for these young people, believers and non-believers, a symbol, a language, for their own resistance to all that was dark and oppressive, all that was centralizing and stifling in the communist regime. The vigil candle became a unique symbol. It was deconstructed by the harsh, utilitarian context to become a religionless symbol. It crossed the boundary between the religious and the religionless. The young people struggled with the reality of the symbol, the paschal story, the Christ event. Perhaps the symbols forced them to confront their own faith story as the symbols of faith began to speak in new ways. The old patterns of prayers had to be rethought, reinvented. And so these young people did not simply identify themselves or their individual stories with the sacred story as they had inherited it. Such identification always runs the risk of possessing or controlling the sacred story. Rather, the story became *for them*. It possessed them, and through them and their obedience and vigilance, it became relevant, meaningful in the politically dangerous, socially oppressive, and environmentally polluted world they knew all too well.

The vigil candle, then, not only represented the light of Christ shining in the darkness; it became a symbol for peace. Because of this negotiation between the young people's faith story and the reality of their communist world, the religious symbol became a symbol for all. The small vigil candle became a sign for peaceful manifestation, peaceful resistance, for, as one pastor explained, when you set out in the chilly October evening with lighted candles to face the soldiers, you have no hands for weapons. One hand holds the candle and the other shields the flickering light from the autumn wind. It was this peaceful procession, streaming forth from the churches, walking out into the streets, gathering people; it was this liturgical procession—a kairos moment or, as Luther would have called it, a gospel shower[10]—that brought down an oppressive political, economic, and social system.

Walking out into the street constituted the climax of this event, but in fact the walking had begun long before. Simply the act of attending these clandestine prayers in the late seventies and early eighties was a dangerous rupture of one's everyday routine. It could have meant imprisonment. Those involved could have experienced, and often did, reprisals or loss of benefits at work. Young people often were denied the possibility to study or pursue higher education. But in order to the answer the question "Who is Christ for us today?" these young people were propelled out into the unknown. They did not claim their religious heritage as a privilege that set them apart from the world; they did not regard their baptism as a birthright, but they responded to the challenge of an impossible responsibility, a calling that came to them from the outside. Without even realizing it, as they walked to prayer daily, weekly, or however regularly, they entered into the waters to be drowned, to become again as Jesus, powerless. Daily they took the risk of living unrehearsed characters, improvising on a stage. What was their weapon? What was their script? Prayer. A simple communal and public prayer. To this prayer and to this forum, all of a sudden, the nonbaptized were also coming. Prayer was at the heart of their life in the world, a prayer that opened a space, a welcome to all. Prayer constituted their witness.

The Holy Spirit's work was not to be seen in any particular religious manifestation, nor in any special calling that these young people assumed (as if they heard an inner voice). No, the Holy Spirit irrupted precisely in the unrehearsed, partial, even unknowing participation in an event, in a work, that could not be defined or even

> **Prayer constituted their witness.**

understood in its happening, for this work was the Holy Spirit's own. Is not the gospel always the surprise of the unrehearsed, the joy of the provisional—an unexpected adventure?

This liturgical manifestation did not mean just personal disruption; it also brought with it institutional disruption. It broke open the doors of the church. Church leaders—Bishop Johannes Hempel of Dresden, Bishop Krusche of Magdeburg, Bishop Schönherr, Probst Falke, Pastor Reinhold Fritz, Superintendent Magarius, Pastor Groeger, Pastor Wonnenberger (and the list could go on)—and many laity who sustained and maintained the prayers knew that the doors of the church had to be open. They knew that the doors had to be open to those who might even betray them. Church leaders allowed the small gatherings to happen in church sanctuaries and basements. Despite their agreement with state authorities to curb political sermons and activities, they still opened up churches for public prayer that gave space to secular society to express itself. Concerns and anguish, the issues of secular life, were welcomed into the church.

Of course, as the prayers grew in size and the discussions became more political, there was fear, but also a deep realization that the gospel continually calls the community to keep the doors open. These small groups of Christians were a form of ecclesia, an assembly or gathering of "those who are called out, without understanding ourselves religiously as privileged, but instead seeing ourselves as belonging wholly to the world," as Bonhoeffer puts it.[11] They listened to the voice, the call of Jesus, but the cry of Jesus was to be heard in their neighbor, in the *other*, regardless of the other's political or religious orientations. Christ became not an object of adoration or of praise, but a Christ disseminated in the world. Their obedience to this Christ began in prayer. It was this prayer, this liturgical resistance, that brought about an equally important and even wider systemic disruption. Through this liturgical event, it was the Holy Spirit acting, disrupting the foundations, the laws, the values of an entire society. Out of faith and with a love as strong as fire, the oppressors, the unjust, and evil itself were consumed.

It is far better to consume those opposed to God with love than with violence, with a meal rather than condemnation. Unfortunately, humankind still resorts to violence, to the burning of books and people, literally and emotionally, publicly and privately. The ultimate disruption came in East Germany with the collapse, with the rupture in the wall of Berlin. What began as a simple communal and public prayer, a baptismal discipline, climaxed in the unexpected rupture of an entire political/cultural system. The powerless means of prayer silences the mighty weapons of nations.

A Different Kind of Knowing

At the beginning of this first chapter I claimed that the spiritual life is surprisingly not about *me*. Rather, the spiritual life is being part of God's act of reclaiming the world, being part of God's initiative of reconciling all humanity and creation to God and God's plan for this world. The spiritual life is being inserted into that plan of reconciliation. Rather than me being the center or finding a balance within myself, I discover that along with others, in prayer and in community, a continually new way is set out before me.

This way, however, is at best only partly visible; in fact, it may be primarily invisible. The wisdom of the cross, Luther writes, "is so completely hidden that only God knows the way of the righteous. To even the righteous themselves, it is hidden."[12] The spiritual path, this way on which I am led, is full of the unexpected and is often covered up under its opposite. What appears to be a dead end turns out to be the unexpected way the Holy Spirit has chosen to create something new. Living this spiritual adventure, living in the unexpected, is living a provisionality—that is, living with great freedom to continually respond and interact with others in and out of community, nimble, flexible, attentive. Luther, reflecting on Psalm 1 (using the Vulgate translation), writes about the spiritual path as a way known primarily by God: "For the Lord knows the way of the righteous, but the way of the ungodly will pass away."[13] This way is often hidden to me, even if I am the one on the path, but the way is known completely by God. Psalm 1 sets two ways before humankind. These ways are described by Luther as the way of believers and the way of the ungodly (defined as those who think badly about God): "Hold these two always as opposites: Faith in God and ungodliness, God's Law and human counsel."[14] The way of the righteous consists simply in faith, faith as a different type of knowing and acting.

This way, according to the psalm, consists of a simple activity: meditating on God's law, day and night. Luther amends a particular word in the Latin of Psalm 1:2. The Latin text reads: "But his will is with the law of the Lord, and he will meditate on his law, day and night." And Luther translates: "*Sondern hat Lust zum Gesetz des Herrn und redet von seinem Gesetz Tag und Nacht,*" which is close to the NRSV: "But their delight is in the law of the Lord, and on his law they meditate day and night." Luther, however, translates *meditate* with the word *redet*, or "speaks." For the moment, though, I will focus on the German word *Lust* (delight).

The way of the righteous, the way of faith—this hidden way—is experienced and grows through feeling delight, wonder, and even desire. All of these describe meditation. God's law draws me into itself, and it entices me along the way. It awakens delight and sweetness and joy, even if that is a quiet, simple joy. Deep emotions are shaped within me by the Holy Spirit through this encounter with God's law/word. Deep affections arise out of an encounter with Christ.[15] They are the response to this encounter, a response that cannot be captured in words or be clearly seen. These affections then lead one, together with the gathered assembly, out into action, out into the streets to encounter many neighbors. "Moreover, because the Holy Spirit is received through faith, consequently hearts are renewed and endowed with new affections so as to be able to do good works," as the Augsburg Confession says.[16]

These affections attest to a different type of knowing, a unique, unspoken, unrecognized communion. Connectivity does not describe this communion. "Feeling connected" places everything around me in relationship to me. *I* remain the subject even when I'm connected to others. Whereas this communion can be characterized as a space holding something latent within it,[17] this latency cannot be described. It is known only by its impact, by something that returns or resurfaces in communion pointing to its center, Jesus. Jesus continually returns and is the source of this communion. Perhaps it is best described as being held by an indefinable center, by Jesus, who continually returns (in a meal). Delight in God's word, as a unique way of knowing, points me to something latent, something that cannot be defined or captured in experience. The new affections that characterize this knowing are themselves an expression of a shared trauma deep in every experience. They point to a latency, to something irresistible in the encounter, in the word. At the same time, in every experience, this latency pushes me further and further into communion. These affections, and this latency, inherently belong to what I will call a spiritual journey, one that takes me deeper into that encounter, into the impact of the Christ event.[18]

Deep affections and emotions play a crucial role in Luther's theology. He understands human beings according to the Hebraic sense of heart. Birgit Stolt has wonderfully demonstrated the important role that the heart plays in Luther's theology. The heart is the seat of both thoughts and emotions, she writes, the "spiritual perception-function of humans, the innermost center of personality. Heart and understanding are insolubly bound to one another."[19] Stolt quotes Luther's translation of Isaiah 6:10 from the Bible edition of 1545 (in other words, the older Luther is being quoted, not the young, naive, overly monastic Luther): *"Verstocke das Herz dieses Volkes / und lass ihre Ohren dicke sein / und blende ihre Augen / Dass sie nicht sehen mit ihren Augen / noch hören mit ihren Ohren / noch verstehen mit ihrem Herzen / und sich bekehren und genesen."*[20] (My translation: "Harden the hearts of the people, stop their ears and shut their eyes so that they cannot see with their eyes or hear

> Deep affections and emotions play a crucial role in Luther's theology.

with their ears or comprehend with their hearts and turn and heal." The NRSV replaces "heart" with "mind" in both occurrences.) The heart understands. Intelligence and affections are not divided.

Young Luther's own struggle had been as much with what God's righteousness meant cognitively (was it simply retributive justice or mercy?) as with his deep-seated emotions, his strong revulsion occasioned by words that presented him with a very calculating and retributive God.[21] Or, perhaps more accurately, Luther's struggle was of the heart: to know God (to recognize, to discern, to feel, even physically to know)[22] is to experience God on all levels of one's existence, through the mind, emotions, and body. God, in addressing the totality of one's being, draws one even more deeply into a relationship where one finally moves, as Luther did, from hating (a strong emotion) the idea of God's righteousness or justice to finding it sweet. When I have tasted this sweetness, I want more.

Luther also uses the example of sweet wine: "This Word is delicious Malvasier wine and living sap," he writes, still commenting in the latter part of his life on Psalm 1 and the meaning of delight in God's law.[23] The word draws me in, like sweet wine, and after I have tasted it, I do not desire anything else. It is normal, Luther continues, that when I have tasted such fine wine, I will not want to go back to water or lite beer![24] The heart experiences righteousness, reconciliation, an immeasurable goodness latent within the fibers of creation and history. This latency has a wonderful taste, sweetness, and delight that cannot be totally defined. Luther uses the word *Wohlgefallen*—it is well, and it falls comfortably into place, as it should be. Faith, that which the Holy Spirit alone writes on hearts, is awakened, nurtured, and increased. In this sweetness, judgment is turned to mercy; righteousness and peace kiss each other (Ps 85:10); obedience becomes a joy-filled expression of faith, a gospel attribute. A quiet, serene joy permeates everyday struggles. The experience of the sweetness of the word, the beginnings of knowing God in the heart, is the mark of a baptismal spirituality and the beginnings of a communion, of being Christian, of bearing one another.

When the heart is the seat of both intellect and affect, I become aware of the many ways in which words and expressions, thoughts and emotions, work together. Language itself is formed through the experience of listening, through the presence of others in communication and in communion. As human beings, all enter into a world of words and emotions that mutually affects and forms them. My own thoughts, affections, and words are shaped by the thoughts, affections, and words of many around me. I am immediately involved in a very basic form of communality. This molding into a community happens in a particular and unique way in the Psalms, for the Psalms show me the heart of the saints, how they spoke and prayed, how they struggled with and rejoiced in God. The heart, words, prayer, and affections of the saints give me a language, forming a communion with them.

Am I now advocating for the imitation of the saints? Protestants in particular, following the example of the early Reformers (both German and Swiss), have learned not to venerate or pray to the saints. Despite the stern warnings against imitating holy examples, everyone seems nonetheless quick to fashion contemporary idols, whether they be gifted preachers, teachers, or singers. The cult of the person—even the person of faith—is alive and well among us. We like to follow "monks wearing red pants," Luther notes.[25]

The Psalms, however, offer a much different example—not constraining and oppressive examples that dictate a way of life that I can never imitate or follow ("Oh, how will ever be like her?"), nor a "guru-makes-disciples" example, but a liberating example. Liberating because the Psalms do not just tell stories about the saints; they place me in the heart of the saints, praying and singing, speaking and walking, weeping and rejoicing, seeing and tasting the sweetness of God. In the Psalms I encounter how the saints struggled with God, with friends and enemies, and how they stood in the midst of danger and suffering. I see how they spoke with God. I see their heart, "the most inner treasure of their soul."[26] I see the foundation and source of their words and works,entering into their heart, which addresses, speaks, interrogates, resonates, and molds experience, embedding you and me in this communion of believers. The words, the struggles, and the joys are shared in a unique communion. The heart of the saints also confronts me; that is, at times I experience their heart—their words, their affections—as an assault, a confusing and disruptive encounter.

Luther points to this unique communion in his introduction to the Psalter (1528 and 1545):[27] the Psalms give the holiest of the holy, Jesus, and what he has done along with all the saints as they still are doing it.[28] In other words, the Psalms do not only give a word from the past but a word that is an event today, becoming today. The prayer is placed in the heart of Jesus and with all the saints, through all time, with all believers in a unique communion. Jesus redefines both context and subject; Jesus i establishes the contours of this communion. The human heart discovers that it is not alone but always in relation. This is in fact a basic characteristic of creation itself. "There is not a tree," Luther comments on Psalm 1:3, "that produces fruit for itself, rather it gives its fruit for others." In this one can see that all creation upholds the law of love.[29] When I am decentered, I discover—through others, through creation, through art and song and the myriad human expressions in culture—dimensions of life that I had never dreamed possible. I am created with and for the other. I am created for a companionship. I am created for community, for a communion. Unlike the legends of saints or the cult of religious pop stars today, the Psalms embed me in a communion. The hearts revealed in the Psalms are hearts intimately shaped by the divine, touched, marked, tattooed by God and by the neighbor. Through this communion, I become a free, willing, and spontaneous follower of Christ.[30] Together, the community freely and joyfully obeys God's word and fulfills God's commandments; it is a people who take time to rest and to work, who can enjoy the day of spiritual rest and not fear the night of work, a people young and not so young who, for example, dare to gather in prayer secretly, to praise and thank and plead with God.

Jesus establishes the contours of this communion.

You and I are called to pay more attention to this shaping, this spirituality, through prayer. These examples and this communion are to be taken seriously, Bonhoeffer argues, both in the Psalms and in daily life: "[The church] will have to see that it does not underestimate the significance of the human 'example' (which has its origin in the humanity of Jesus and is so important in Paul's writings); the church's word gains weight and power not through concepts but by example."[31]

In this book, the underground prayer groups in East Germany and especially in Leipzig will be such an example, a modern-day Psalter. Some shy away when speaking about examples that involve a cross, for the cross evokes images of suffering, torture, and cruelty. These images of the cross they want to reject, just as a God who demands such suffering is to be rejected.[32] To the contrary, what I have discovered on this journey into a baptismal spirituality is that the cross continually surfaces in life in surprising and life-giving ways, not as violence. The tree of death is really the tree of life. The Christ event, the paschal event, is not only the cross but the life, death, and resurrection of Jesus. Because of the Christ event, suffering will not have the last word. Faith communities attempt to remember and ritualize this originary event in worship and through prayer. Yet, as this event continually returns, I begin to realize that I never will be able to control or master it. In fact, the iterations of worship and prayer attest to this inability, to this event as a question, always pushing the community forward to places and adventures unknown, hidden, and uncomfortable. I am left without words. *Selah*. New beginnings.

At the cross in every life, at the cross in the life of my neighbor, at the cross in the life of a city and society, something latent, something about God, something about life is discovered.

2

Today: Everything Is Different

Today

On a beautiful warm summer afternoon in Leipzig, sitting on a balcony drinking coffee and eating pastry, listening to the birds chirping and the cars driving by in the center of this vibrant city, I was listening to a story by Pastor Wolfgang Groeger. It is one of many stories belonging to the events of fall 1989, when the wall of Berlin came tumbling down.

> You can't believe the fear we had on October 9 [1989]. ["*Es ist ein tief gehendes Erlebnis*": It is a deeply penetrating experience.] We knew something would happen. But we didn't know what would happen. I have two teenage daughters and, as we were sitting at the breakfast table, I said to them, "You better stay at home this evening."

And they responded, "No, we are going." What a crazy, scary thing when you don't know if you will see one another again in the evening. I cannot speak anymore about this in public lectures. The tears well up. I cannot help it. That afternoon, I was at the Michaeliskirche. In the evening, the church was full to the rafters. People were flowing over into the street.

Three things happened during the prayer that evening, three strong experiences. I don't remember the sermon; it wasn't one of the three! The first happening was the arrival of Bishop Johannes Hempel. He didn't come often to Leipzig. Leipzig gave him too many problems! But in these days, he was present, and he went to all six churches where the prayers for peace were being held. He spoke in all six churches, and what he said was incredibly important for us all: whoever attacks you attacks the whole church. In other words, if the soldiers attack tonight, they are not attacking just some fringe group, or one little parish, some isolated group. No, they are attacking the body of Christ.

The second happening was near the end of the prayer. Dr. Zimmerman, who was part of the Committee of Six [a group of leaders in Leipzig who joined together to advocate for a nonviolent approach to the manifestations], came and spoke again about the peaceful approach that all were to take as they went into the street. He too had visited all six churches. He was the last one to speak. Soon after, the prayer per se ended,

and then everyone left and walked out into the street.
In the meantime, we were waiting in the church. Everything had been prepared at Michaeliskirche to welcome
the wounded and care for them. We would do this all
in the church. Then I remembered that Dr. Zimmerman liked smoking cigarillos. And I said to him, I need
a cigarillo!

Then the third happening occurred. Our organist
came to me. He was a very upright and faithful man. He
came to me and said, "Pastor, today everything is different."[1] Selah.

After this, we too went into the street and joined the
tens of thousands who were circling the city.

The miracle happened that evening in Leipzig. The city was
surrounded by tanks and soldiers, but no shots were fired. The
peaceful demonstration continued to walk, to pilgrim through the next few weeks, increasing in size until finally, unexpectedly, the whole Eastern Bloc shook and walls crumbled.

A little while later in our conversation, Pastor Groeger noted, "We can't pinpoint any particular source to this event. What we lived was a *kairos* moment. At a particular time, at a particular place, a very particular event happened: This was Pentecost in Jerusalem, or the walls of Jericho tumbling down. We lived this *kairos* in 1989.

> The miracle happened that evening in Leipzig. The city was surrounded by tanks and soldiers, but no shots were fired.

Throughout the 1980s, with its weapon escalation on both sides of the East German border, we could never have imaged that this threat would disappear. We could never have imagined or prepared for what happened."

Selah

Today everything is different. (*Heute ist alles anderes.*) Selah.

With that one little word, selah, with that biblical summation that Pastor Groeger uttered at the end of his story, I was ushered into the indescribability of a particular historical moment, into something latent in history that continually resurfaces in different and unexpected ways. The story cannot be archived; it cannot be recorded or made sense of; it only can be told, liturgically, over and over again. Yet, it is as if in each encounter, in each telling, part of the Holy Spirit's mystery that works continually throughout history, and through lives—my life, your life—is secretly, quietly, unexpectedly creating and revealing and nurturing itself in the fabric of history, in each person, and in community.

Selah is a curious word that opens and closes doors. When a faith community sings the Psalms in worship (if they are sung at all), the worshipping community isn't usually confronted by this curious word that appears a bit haphazardly throughout the Psalter. It erupts in many places. In Psalm 46, on which the hymn "A Mighty Fortress" is based, it appears three times: once after verse 3 ("Though its waters roar and foam, though the mountains tremble with its tumult. Selah."), and once after verses 7 and 11 ("The Lord of hosts is with us; the God of Jacob is our refuge. Selah."). Luther, the Old Testament professor and translator, couldn't figure it out. Finally, he writes, "The word s*elah* is introduced confusedly and altogether without discernable order, to show that the motion of the Spirit is secret, unknown to us, and by no means possible to be foreseen." He continues, "Wherever it comes, it requires us to omit the words of the psalms"—in other words, it interrupts the words of the psalms, it breaks into the words, and we are brought to a "pausing and quiet frame."[2]

Selah interrupts our reading, our meditation, our life. It disrupts the meanings we want to construct. It breaks through the mighty walls of identity, of culture, of institutions, of theory. *Selah* silences us and all our constructions. This little word, a singular expression, is the Spirit's trace; it is an utterance that shook the foundations of a particular understanding of church in the late medieval period; it reversed forms of superstition; it broke down the walls of a gray socialist society in East Germany, the walls of Stasi oppression and forced conformity, the walls of despondency in a totalitarian system. Inside other walls—the walls of Western society, trusting in arms buildup, in weapons and in the weapon industry, in superior power and technology, in consumerism and in wealth—*selah* is heard as a sigh, if it is heard at all.

Selah. Something suddenly becomes possible. A singular utterance is heard: one word, one small group praying, one voice crying, one bright vigil candle, a few fearful people stepping out in the chilly autumn evening.

Commenting on a text in Isaiah, Luther writes,

Isaiah 30:15–16 says: "In silence and in hope shall your strength be. But you have said, 'By no means, but we will take refuge with horses.'" That is, with physical assistance, in worldly battle, without the name of the Lord. The saints, however, are in silence and patience and in hope, not physical activity, like those people, for they are saved by the name of the Lord. This does not come about except in hope and patience and silence, whereas the ungodly seek to be saved in bustle and physical activity, indeed by the vanity of physical activity.[3]

The list of such physical activities is endless, from building walls to amassing weapons, fighting wars, and demanding conformity (imposing identities—cultural, economic, and gendered). It takes place too when people construct dogmatic towers, perfect systems such as Babel, blind to the ensuing exclusions and confusion. Too often power is preferred and silence avoided. Physical and emotional violence (even abuse) is favored. People trust in their own power and myths (patriotic or white supremacist or other human fabrications) rather than trust in the name of the Lord.

Too often, power is preferred and silence avoided.

Those who wish to take refuge with horses, who wish to construct their own tower, who wish to control the contours of their life and its history, believe that they can find fulfillment, wholeness—the meaning of life—in that construction. The incomplete and unfulfilled is to be avoided, the partial is to be shunned, for it only points to brokenness, to inability. The partial makes *me* uncomfortably vulnerable, apparently incomplete.

But as I hope you will see, the story of the clandestine and not-so-clandestine prayer groups in East Germany in the autumn of 1989 witnesses that which is hidden within history and which, as unique and singular, cannot be repeated but continually calls out to become *for us* today. It calls everyone it touches to dwell in silence, selah. It calls to a responsibility that is always vulnerable. It calls to what seems like an impossible responsibility. One is called to an attentiveness to a singular moment and to its cry, knowing that this moment does not contain within itself—that history does not contain within itself—the ultimate answer to the quest for meaning. I will not find the meaning of life within the confines of my life, within me, nor within the contexts I inhabit. Rather, every moment, every context, is itself a moment of hope; every moment is the possibility of hope that calls us to vigilance, patience, silence, and action.

Vigilance, as Heinrich Schlier describes it, "signifies an attention to the surprising and decisive situation even if it appears as something normal or rational. . . . It signifies listening to the call of the Spirit, which resounds throughout history as a call to love and to total availability. . . . It is at the same time a realism: Finding oneself day after day confronted with the extreme possibility of history and hearing the call of Christ, which is rejected by history, we go beyond any illusion we might have about history. We will no longer dream about directing history."[4]

Vigilance is an obedience to the historical moment, the discipline to live in a singular moment, attentive to God's future—present in every event. This obedience demands patience, living the moment for and from God, dwelling in that which is partial—the moon can only be half-seen, *"und ist doch rund und schön!"* (and yet is round and beautiful!)[5]—waiting for the Lamb to open and read the book of life, trusting. Selah.

The only one worthy to reveal the mystery of God is the Lamb (Rev 5; 10). This one, Jesus Christ, is the one who entered history, took on the human condition, and lived it fully (not as an intruder or stranger or passerby, but as incarnate, in the flesh). The infinite fully dwelling in the finite. The mystery at the heart of life—God's mystery embedded in history—that singular event and struggle will be revealed, but now I am asked to wait in silence. The mystery of God, that originary history that no narrative can recount in words (or narrative or sermon) but which resonates to the ends of the earth, is experienced as a silent, unexpected, unassuming event; a prayer, perhaps; an utterance of the Spirit. Selah.

> Day to day pours forth speech,
>> and night to night declares knowledge.
> There is no speech, nor are there words;
>> their voice is not heard;
> yet their voice goes out through all the earth,
>> and their words to the end of the world. (Ps 19:2–4)

"There is no speech . . . yet their voice goes out through all the earth." And in that silent utterance, in that absent manifestation that only faith grasps,[6] liberation is experienced. Living in the partial, living in vigilance, living attentive to the irruption of

the Spirit in any and every moment, frees me from the obses-
sion to possess, to control, to direct. All of a sudden, I find
myself in a new grammatical framework: God is the subject, not
me! The freedom of no longer being the subject allows me to
encounter a different history within the boundaries of the many
histories human beings attempt to write and define. God acts.
God "makes wars cease to the end of the earth; [God] breaks
the bow, and shatters the spear; [God] burns the shields with
fire" (Ps 46:9). But God does this in such a way that no one
can take credit for it. (Though the media and journalists and
bloggers always will be tempted to pinpoint the causes for such
liberation.) Others might perhaps notice the event's singularity,
its very provisional nature of here today and gone tomorrow,
and dismiss it as a rare occurrence without ongoing impact. Yet
God is continually creating, bringing forth God's dominion,
reclaiming the world to God's self. Surprisingly, God does so
provisionally, like a summer thunderstorm suddenly drenching
the earth in rain and just as quickly dissipating before the bright,
hot sun—creating time and again a today in which everything is
unexpectedly different.

"Be still . . . and know that I am God! I am exalted among
the nations, I am exalted in the earth" (Ps 46:10). Selah.

Unexpected Ways

In that singular moment in Leipzig in 1989, as Pastor Groeger
and a few others watched, young and not-so-young walked out of
the church to form a huge procession in the streets, not knowing

what they would encounter, the only word they could live from was this untranslatable word from the Psalms: selah.

In moments of heightened tension, when no way forward can be seen, when there is nothing to rely on but on a community of faith, equally fearful and yet still equally believing, history changes course. The unexpected shift takes place on both a historical scale and an individual scale, of course. I remember one night in Olomouc (Olomóc) in the mid-1980s. The former Czechoslovakia was under oppressive communist rule. It was late, approaching midnight, and I was in a car taking me to a clandestine meeting with a priest who was under house arrest. The priest risked leaving the house to meet with me not only to have contact with another person of faith, but to be part of that larger community of faith that extends beyond borders.

Three other young men were in the car with me. Suddenly, we were stopped by the police. Where were four men going in the middle of the night? It dawned on me then what a crazy plan this was. No one traveled this late at night in a highly controlled society, and certainly not in a group. I quickly whispered to the driver that, on top of everything else, I didn't have my papers with me (also a crime). The policeman began checking the IDs of my three companions. Everyone knew that when the police discovered that I was a foreigner, they would all land in prison. All I could do was sit and wait and sing silently in my heart Psalm 121, "I lift up my eyes to the hills—from where will my help come? My help comes from the Lord, who made heaven and earth."

Over and over again, I sang the whole psalm as the police noted everyone's information. Then they asked for my papers.

Before I could say anything, the driver, in a rather nonplussed tone, explained, "He doesn't have them." All of sudden, it was as if I did not exist. The policeman did not ask me one question, which would have immediately revealed my foreign origin, as I could not speak Czech. It was as if I had vanished. The policeman turned away and let us drive on into the night. The driver and my companions sat for a moment in complete disbelief. What had just happened? They didn't linger over the question too long, though.

> The policeman turned away and let us drive on into the night.

There was no logical or historical explanation to this event, to the fact that I had become literally invisible in the eyes of the policeman. Later, in Prague, I asked an elder of the underground church, Jiri Kaplan, what he made of it. He looked at me and said, "But Dirk, don't you remember the story of Peter led out of prison by the angel, walking past the first and second guards, who did not see him?" (Acts 12).

Of course, I wanted to find explanations. I wanted to figure out what happened. I wanted to devise my own solution, create a plan, and write a history. When I do write such a history, I usually credit myself and my own ability or prowess. But the history that the Spirit is writing does not conform to my ideas or narratives or desires. The history the Holy Spirit writes is a hidden history, an invisible history, a silent history that runs like an underground river below and through the chaos, the stress, the competition, the jostling and seductions, the violence, and the injustice of this world. An originary history—God's reclaiming of the world to God's self—continually attempts to rise to the surface. This mystery can only be experienced, not learned in books or programs. It is experienced suddenly, unexpectedly, provisionally, disruptively, and in life-giving ways.

And always in the everyday. The underground prayers in East Germany were obviously not, in their beginnings, huge public events. For a long time, they existed as small groups of people gathered in apartments or quietly in churches. People interrupted the schedule of their highly ordered and routinized lives to participate, to risk of gathering for prayer. They took the time to light the vigil candle. Taking the risk of silence, living into the selah, happened first of all in very ordinary ways such as gathering to share, discuss, and pray together. But the ordinary soon became the extraordinary.

Practices of ordinary, everyday life can offer a glimpse into the Holy Spirit's working. French Jesuit philosopher and theologian Michel de Certeau writes, "If it is true that the grid of 'discipline' is everywhere becoming clearer and more extensive, it is all the more urgent to discover how an entire society resists being reduced to it."[7] The discipline he refers to is the discipline that a society, a culture, imposes on its adherents. People are constantly being pressured into forms of behavior. What a society values, likes, and dislikes is shaped by industries, commercial sports, and entertainment. The imagination is molded by metanarratives that ignore the dispossessed or write out of existence slavery and its ongoing impact. Language is forced into conformity through the hyperbolic conversations found on sitcoms. Gender roles are artificially shaped.[8] Education is driven by the god of assessment. For those belonging to communities of faith, even the vision of church and faith is affected by the pressures of culture.

Society disciplines its members into conformity, recognized or not. Yet, in the midst of the imposition of cultural, economic, and political identities, a silent resistance is offered, sometimes unknowingly. This resistance does not consist of public demonstrations, marching down the street to city hall, or being overtly confrontational—all valuable forms of resistance. Resistance can be as simple as refusing to live according to the rhythms of societal and cultural impositions. It happens in everyday life when a family decides to take time weekly to respect Sabbath, a time of rest, or as they replace militarized toys for more creative inspirations that embody different values. It happens when someone decides to cook their meals without processed food and then invites guests over. It happens when someone refuses to send text messages while in a face-to-face conversation (and perhaps even turns off their device during worship). Such resistance happens even when someone goes out walking and chooses where they walk, how they walk, and with whom they engage.

De Certeau classified many of these activities as he encountered them in the late twentieth century. They may be hidden or silent, singular and plural, devious and tricky, or simply stubborn.[9] The hidden and stubborn practices are perhaps those that most appropriately describe the prayers in East Germany. Begun clandestinely, hidden from view, people gathered in small groups in each other's apartments (or in the case of young people, in their parents' apartments). They did not attempt anything new or radical. They read from Scripture, held silence, prayed, perhaps lighted a candle, and quietly talked about what was threatening life in their society and what was burdening them. The practice brought in people from all walks of life and all their experiences. People, when they left these prayer gatherings, went out and walked again, looking and hearing and engaging vigilantly, attentively, in hope. They were hidden and stubborn in this practice—is, persistent, rooted in an ancient pattern of prayer made vibrant by its intersection with life.

Surreptitiously, yet tenaciously, they set out in a new way,[10] focusing not on what must be preserved or what might be most attractive or successful, but simply staying vigilant to that which was most urgent for their time. This new way is surprisingly not one that can be constructed. Rather, it is one that is discovered. This new way is one that the Holy Spirit continually traces, a hidden way that requires both vigilance and patience, silence and action, an attentive obedience to the simplest and most ordinary tasks of life. I believe a certain forbearance shaped the way in which people engaged the prayers. They embodied a restraint that was characterized by vigilance to the context around them and by a deep obedience to the messiness of life, both its joys and its struggles. Obedience must be understood not as submission but as self-control exercised in kindness, gentleness, and overall in love. This obedience is joyful. It is drawn forward by something unknown, something it cannot easily name or understand.

The fruit of the Spirit emerges and reveals this new way that God works within all creation, reconciling and building up. Perhaps eyes and ears need training to hear, see, and seek something very different in the events and practices that make up both daily life and the community of faith.

The vigilant, hopeful ones desire that which is hidden: the pearl among many valueless stones, the hidden word, the law of God, the voice of God resonating deep in the heart of creation. They don't seek half-heartedly or haphazardly. They don't attempt to accomplish great works while missing the simplest, most self-evident ones. "Whoever is faithful in a very little is faithful also in much; and whoever is dishonest in a very little is dishonest also in much" (Luke 16:10). In the most insignificant task faithfully accomplished lies hidden the most costly, precious gift. "Just as the treasure in a field is hidden, so is the prize of obedience hidden in the rejected and despised command."[11]

> This obedience is joyful. It is drawn forward by something unknown, something it cannot easily name or understand.

The obedience of faith rises up from delight, from the joy of finding the treasure in the field. I run and sell all I possess in order to buy that field. All those incomplete desires and pursuits begin to vanish. My relationship to life, to the people and the things around me, shifts from possessiveness to thanksgiving. I give myself over to the beauty of this field. Isn't this what Luther means when he writes, "*Aber Gott will nicht Opfer, sondern Gehorsam*"?[12]—God does not want sacrifice, but obedience. Sacrifice, however, is an old inclination, always wanting to do something.

Faithfulness and obedience walk together, as Bonhoeffer points out. God's word draws one into this obedience, which defines the life of a believer. Obedience is not a work one painstakingly attempts to accomplish but a gift of the Holy Spirit, who alone knows the new way. Obedience is living in faith. Obedience is a child of faith. The faithful are obedient. In obedience, the new way can be perceived, if only partially.

An Adventure in Prayer

How does God's word draw me into obedience, into a new way? The story of the prayers in East Germany reveal one possible answer: a Christian life and prayer inform each other. These young Christians lived lives rooted in prayer, shaped by the language of prayer, the language of Scripture, read, sung, discussed, chewed on during worship: a true adventure in prayer. Prayer comes to life in the very choices that the faith community makes: What type of toys will our children play with? What are the community's meal-sharing habits? How and with whom? And so forth. In these simple, everyday choices rooted in prayer, the Spirit offers the goodness of God's way. The God of peace is a God who works reconciliation in through the many different ways that the baptized live out this simple obedience of prayer.

Yet, for some reason, the tendency is still to create a divide between what is spiritual and what is routine, or what some might call secular or profane. I've already noted how, in the spiritual quest, body and spirit often are separated. Civil life and religious life are dissociated. Such division has consequences. Some will run the risk of overspiritualizing daily things, endowing daily practices with a value that they cannot hold. Daily practices, even wholeheartedly engaged, cannot bring lasting fulfillment. Some people talk about reaching a deep communion through certain daily things without regard or thought to suffering or to what certain practices may mean in terms of exclusion and oppression for others. Is there a spirituality of coffee if people are exploited in its production?

The quest for a spirituality can keep people stuck in their self-centered identities. It can simply be another tool or method used to bridge the gap between a secular and a sacred reality (no matter how the sacred reality is defined, whether residing deep within or in some transcendent realm), leaving me quite comfortable in my secular. On the contrary, for those who engaged in the underground prayers, spirituality was not such a bridge that allowed them to escape the constraints of their daily routines and oppressions.

Realizing how easily the human spirit can spiritualize its own desire (thereby not risking its own life), the underground prayer groups took this initial lesson (the deep connection between prayer and action) one step further. Spirituality is neither spiritualization nor escape. Communal prayer led to a procession, literally walking out into the street. Not a procession where people "want only to see and to be seen,"[13] but a procession that was prayer itself, pleading to God for protection and for cleansing the air—not of evil spirits and demonic forces, as Luther observed in the early sixteenth century, but literally cleansing the air of Leipzig, which knew the worst smog in the former German Democratic Republic. The procession took prayer out into the street, for the street, and with the street.

In Luther's early sermon on prayer and procession in Holy Week, he writes about the proper use of processions: "First, that God may graciously protect the crops in the fields and cleanse the air—not only that God may send blessed rain and good weather to ripen the fruit, but rather that the fruit may not be poisoned."[14] Taking one's prayer out into the world, literally, physically, moving with warm bodies into the fields and singing and reading the gospel in the outside air, was for Luther a means of cleansing. Of course, today that enchanted world is one of the past (as described by Charles Taylor).[15] It was a world that believed pestilence and other plagues came "from the evil spirits who poison the air and then also the fruit, wine, and grain," as Luther puts it.[16] Rather than prayer being a feel-good activity, a magical hotline, or a performance, prayer can be understood as a solidarity with the world—people and all creation. The worshipping community also may intuit that prayer has something to do with bodies, with hands outstretched, with heads bowed down or raised up, with bodies kneeling or even prostrate, with bodies dancing and making music and walking, yes, with processions out into the world.

In this life, of course, I don't think that a person is ever really free of self-centered searching. In the clandestine prayers, however, personal egos always may have been present, but they also ceded to a goodness offered to one another and to the neighbor.

Communal prayer had the neighbor at the center, and the neighbor—known or unknown, friend or potential threat (secret police or informer)—could only be met in a spirit of openness, of welcome. The spirituality that emerged in these prayers was first and foremost not spirituality for me (or about me), but for the world. Something of the Holy Spirit disrupts my center. An unexpected new way is revealed that displaces the way I had imagined. From this prayer, the participants went out into the street, vigilant, attentive, hopeful, and offering in their own lives a gospel goodness. Selah.

> Communal prayer had the neighbor at the center.

God's Hidden Way

For those involved in the prayer groups, there was nothing new in what they did. They might even say nothing miraculous happened. This was not an experiment in a new church-growth model or the enactment of a newly invigorated spirituality. There was only faithfulness expressed through communal prayer, faithfulness, for some, to their baptism. In their obedience together, they freely, willingly, and spontaneously found themselves following Christ out into the street.

Reflecting on the role of worship and prayer in a religionless context, Bonhoeffer notes (see pp. 32–33) that being *ekklēsia* has nothing to do with a privileged religiosity (finding security or feeling superior because of established religious practice or tradition). It has nothing to do with making oneself feel good through different spiritual practices. It has all to do with belonging to the world, being present in the midst of a religionless world and all of its struggles.

Prayer in the heart of society, in the heart of the world, is a prayer with open doors, prayer as generous welcome and keen vigilance, prayer as inner renewal and as resistance. The Holy Spirit, who shapes a life of faith through prayer, turns the believer around. This prayer, flowing out into the streets, witnesses and embodies a new creation, a new relationship between God and us in which *I* am no longer the center.

Christian prayer cannot be lived apart from the world around us. Christ is no longer an object that is placed on the walls of churches and chapels. Christ himself is fully immersed in creation: God disseminated and scattered throughout the world, particularly in its suffering. God's dissemination in the world, the cross present in so many situations and events, raises a question that Bonhoeffer already asked: Who is Christ for us today? If Christ is not the object of religion, if Christ is not the object of our worship, but still the one (truly Lord) who shapes our lives in this world, then what does this mean for prayer and for our rituals?[17]

> **Christian prayer cannot be lived apart from the world around us.**

For many pastors living under the communist regime in East Germany, this was the central question about Christ. Pastor Groeger shared, "Resistance wasn't really a theme for us. We didn't talk about resistance, but about Bonhoeffer's question: Who is Jesus Christ for us in this place? This is the question that we kept trying to figure out." The gospel asks a simple question, but it has deeply resounding implications for people, community, and society.

Pastor Groeger continued, "Some themes were important for us: What does the first commandment—you are to have no other gods—mean? We also talked about Romans 13: Is this current state from God or not? How do I act within this state? How do I live within this state?" The questions those believers asked had to do with their faith and how it relates to neighbors and the state.

Scripture provides some surprising directions in trying to figure out this question. Contrary to the world, which turns God into an object, blaming and rejecting God for the violence in the world; contrary to a brand of religiosity, which also turns God into an object, looking to God to solve its problems, looking to God when in distress, expecting God to use God's power— contrary to all these, the Bible, as Bonhoeffer understands it, "directs to God's powerlessness and suffering."[18] The Bible directs us precisely not to a mythical and distant God, but to God born in a manger and executed on a cross, to God powerless and suffering.

In Bonhoeffer's time in Nazi Germany, the church, the community of faith, had fallen into the trap of privilege. It had squandered its call, its mission. It could make no claim on God's revelation. He writes: "We gave away the word and sacraments wholesale; we baptized, confirmed, and absolved a whole nation unasked and without condition. . . . But the call to follow Jesus in the narrow way was hardly ever heard. . . . [Yet] happy are they who, knowing the [costly] grace [of Christ], can live in the world without being of it, who, by following Jesus Christ, are so assured of their heavenly citizenship that they are truly free to live their lives in this world."[19]

Bonhoeffer found himself as a church leader and theologian in opposition to the church, living a life of resistance, living on the margins. Here he discovered that the question "Who is Christ for us today?" is asked not from a place of privilege but from the edge, the outskirts, the margins, from outside the city walls. God's revealing voice was to be heard in the street, in the often-religionless realities that define people's lives.

God's powerlessness and suffering, witnessed in Scripture, is also witnessed and embodied in the life of communities of faith. In fact, deep in the tradition from which Bonhoeffer draws much of his theological thinking, Luther already described the marks of a community of faith, or, as they have come to be known, marks of the church. There are seven marks, which Luther enumerated slightly differently throughout his life. In a later list (1539), he defined these marks as the word preached; baptism; the sacrament of the altar, or Holy Communion; the office of the keys (confession and forgiveness); ministry; prayer and thanksgiving; and bearing the suffering of the neighbor (the "holy possession" of the cross).[20] Communities of faith are precisely defined through certain practices, but rather curious or paradoxical ones, because they are in themselves powerless vis-à-vis the world and they often entail suffering.

I say paradoxical, because who would have thought that in a religionless or secular context an answer to the question "Who is Christ for us today?" would be found at the heart of that which is inherently religious or liturgical (in a sacrament, for example)? The reconfiguration of religious language is disruptive. The religious (powerful, institutional, ritualistic) is turned on its head. In this reconfiguration, one is surprised to discover that a secular response begins in the powerlessness of baptism, in the powerlessness of resistance to dominate culture—for example, in the powerlessness of a few women and men opposing the Nazi war machine, or of a few who witnessed to the Spirit's hidden way.

The starting point of a response is not up in heaven. It is not somewhere up above the high altar in our sanctuaries. It is not in a Jesus who is an object in my life (a life in which *I* remain the center). It is not in any fundamentalist reading of Scripture (that itself becomes a sort of power or weapon used to impose God on others). It is not in any privilege or claim to truth that I might have. The starting point is found in the powerlessness of these marks of the church that form a community. The modality of God's presence in the world is most clearly encountered in places of powerlessness. The worshipping community is constantly directed to the cry in the street and to the unexplainable, unjust, and useless suffering of our neighbor.

The question "Who is Christ for us today?" is an ontological question: a question about the being of Christ. Curiously, even this question still holds Jesus as an object; it ponders God's being. For Bonhoeffer, however, the question is reshaped by its answer. It becomes a *where* question:[21] Where is Christ, God, the Holy

Spirit, in this world? When Christ is no longer the object of worship, he becomes the subject addressing the community. Christ always addresses it from outside itself. Christ addresses the community and me, both through the community and through the neighbor, through the other, whom it does not know.

Now, if God is in the street and not above our high altars or our lovely sanctuaries or beautiful music and song, then I need to ask more questions: Does spirituality lead me to the neighbor? Are the sacraments serving the neighbor? Does God's action, the work of the Holy Spirit, in worship engage the community in the street? What do these marks of the church, these marks of communion, mean for the world?

> The modality of God's presence in the world is most clearly encountered in places of powerlessness.

Writing from prison, Bonhoeffer observes, "Our church has been fighting during these years only for its self-preservation, as if that were an end in itself. It has become incapable of bringing the word of reconciliation and redemption to humankind and to the world. So the words we used before must lose their power, be silenced, and we can be Christians today in only two ways, through prayer and in doing justice among human beings. All Christian thinking, talking, and organizing must be born anew, out of that prayer and action."[22]

The faith community, rooted in the gospel, rooted in a vision of peace and reconciliation, engages a very simple activity:

meditating on God's law, day and night. The world sees this activity as ineffectual, useless. But the faith community embraces powerless means: prayer and love for neighbor.

Prayer and love for neighbor: this action points always beyond the walls of the community. The life each of us has created for ourselves is disrupted; a new adventure begins. When Christ is no longer an object who can be neatly and conveniently fit into my life, then Christ is the one who continually returns through the events and the people I encounter, disrupting my context (my little world), disrupting my identity as self-invented center, disrupting even my desire. All humanly created chains are cast off, endlessly blown away as chaff on the dry ground. But the joy of this disruption is to discover that the community is on a hidden way.

Searching and engaging, always provisionally, listening and encountering, walking on this way, moving forward not knowing where I am going, faith is tasted in prayer, at the heart of a community vulnerable to the world around it. Faith is nurtured and exercised in prayer, and action as self-made contexts and identities are disrupted. Prayer is, to borrow a phrase from the poor theater, "not a collection of skills but an eradication of blocks" that opens the hidden way of the Holy Spirit.[23]

Luther writes about a theological grammar, a grammar that has God as subject, as actor. The Holy Spirit's hidden way in the world is distinguished from human ways and is the foundation of all ways. "The law of the Spirit is one that is written with no letters at all, published in no words, thought of in no thoughts. On the contrary, it is the living will itself and the life of experience."[24] The hidden way of the Holy Spirit, in and under events, persons, situations, constantly eradicating the blocks, the walls, is never clearly seen. It easily can be dismissed, for this way can only be tasted and obediently followed in faith, day and night, in thanksgiving and in lament. This way is apprehended only in faith, through experience that "delights in God's law and speaks on this law day and night." Selah.

3

Faith and Prayer

Faith and Obedience

At the beginning of his book *Discipleship*, Bonhoeffer famously complains about cheap grace.[1] His argument often has been misunderstood by those who insist on a narrow interpretation of "justification by faith alone" without any regard for what justification implies and how it affects life. Yet, Bonhoeffer's argument may be simply stated in this way: Cheap grace is justification by faith alone as a doctrine, as an idea, as a concept. Costly grace, however, is justification as lived experience—costly not through sacrifice but through faith. Justification itself is the foundation of a spiritual life—that is, a way of life given by God and rooted in God alone. Justification by faith alone implies an obedience, or as Luther puts it, channeling Scripture, "*Aber Gott will nicht Opfer, sondern Gehorsam*" (God does not want sacrifice but obedience).[2]

Here is yet another way of understanding Luther's theological grammar. Cheap grace blurs the distinction between what God does and what I might do. Cheap grace forgets that there are two ways, as outlined in Psalm 1.[3] Cheap grace fits nicely into my life, as I want my life to be. Nothing radically changes. Those who relish in such cheap grace, in justification as a mere idea, turn very quickly in on themselves, turn human precepts into God's law, and turn God into their own image. Such a narrow understanding of justification leads only to judgment, whereas costly grace, justification by faith alone known in experience, leads to service. "Self-justification and judging belong together in the same way that justification by grace and serving belong together."[4]

Why, though, raise the question of cheap and costly grace in a discussion about spirituality and spiritual practices? A spiritual life is rooted in faith—in the work of the Holy Spirit writing a new way through history, writing a new law in hearts—and faith invites one continually into obedience. This is best described by Bonhoeffer in the opening pages of *Discipleship*, when he turns to the parable of the treasure in a field. Discipleship, costly grace, is not a new "work's righteousness." Rather, it is a joyous response to the gospel. Excitedly—freely, spontaneously, willingly—someone leaves everything behind for that treasure in the field. It is perhaps not surprising that Bonhoeffer uses the same parable as Luther does in his first commentary on Psalm 1: "Just as the treasure in a field is hidden, so is the prize of obedience hidden in the rejected and despised command."[5] Costly grace has nothing to do with the law and everything to do with the gospel. The treasure in the field—God's act of making righteous, justification—is latent in the lives of the baptized, in the most ordinary practices and events and persons of everyday life. This gospel reality sets a person off on a journey ever deeper into righteousness.

But why speak about a journey? Isn't the righteousness God imparts complete? Isn't God's verdict of righteousness a total justification that is grasped by faith alone? Of course, in baptism God has made a person "fully and perfectly righteous"—that is, reconciled, at one with God—and yet Luther notes that the baptized are still on a journey: "For we perceive that a [person] who is justified is not yet a righteous [person], but is in the very movement or journey toward righteousness."[6] God's mercy toward a person, God's immeasurable goodness, continually deepens righteousness with them, molding them into ministers of reconciliation, peace, new creation, and bearers of hope who are marked by Christ. Throughout a person's journey in this world, horizons are broadened and new depths are discovered as they live more fully into this righteousness. This journey marks the life of a Christian and, in a nutshell, defines spirituality.

In this world, even if God's mercy, justification by faith alone, leads into the fullness of life, life is still full of contradictions. The question that I ask so often, "How do I live my faith?" is perhaps not the one I should be focusing on. This question still places *me*—my own ego—somehow in the center as subject, and the world or neighbor (and even God) as object. But in a life of faith, everything is turned upside down. Faith itself is not something I possess but something that is poured into each heart by the Holy Spirit as a community hears and speaks and sings and eats and drinks Christ. Faith poured into hearts is a continual, daily activity. Faith comes from the outside to each of us. Such faith is poured into hearts in the midst of the praying community. Faith is the encounter with Jesus Christ in the community and in the neighbor. Faith is received. It establishes a unique relationship in which each individual and the community as a whole become one with Jesus and the communion of saints.

> **Faith is the encounter with Jesus Christ in the community and in the neighbor.**

Faith is a dynamic relationship. Faith is not simply another characteristic that makes up who I am. I am not to ask, "Where does faith fit into my life, my game plan?" No, faith determines the very path I am on, the total context in which I find myself. Faith inundates the heart, the whole person. Faith is not a part of life; it *is* life.

A word that Luther struggles with to describe this process by which faith seeps through one's whole life is the German *annehmen* (and its many forms). Literally, its meanings include "to adopt, to receive, to fulfill, to bring into, and/or to overtake." To translate it with "decide" or even "welcome" still places too much emphasis on what an individual is doing (though I am still obliged to use this word). Whatever word is found, it is always the wrong word; such are the contours of human grammar. When I receive faith, it as if faith adopts me, slowly penetrating and permeating all fibers of my being, even into those places I was not aware existed or that I refused to acknowledge. This adoption is never in my control, for I never can totally capture or contain faith; rather, the Holy Spirit continually works faith into each and every life, conforming a person to Jesus Christ. The Holy Spirit takes on my heart, the deepest recesses of my being, the darkest and most inaccessible regions, and transfigures them. Both the dying to self (the disruption of myself as subject and of my context, the world I've built up around me) and ever new beginnings are held by the Spirit in an outpouring of faith.

It is as if the Spirit places a person in a field with a beautiful treasure. They find themselves in this field, in an enclosure, in a life that God has created and given and in which they have everything they need. "The Lord is my chosen portion and my cup; you hold my lot. The boundary lines have fallen for me in pleasant places; I have a goodly heritage" (Ps 16:5–6). In those boundary lines, in that field, God invites everyone to discover the treasure; God awakens faith. The discovery of faith—a sudden joyous moment—sends them off to sell all their possessions (Matt 13:44). This moment is like an apocalypse; it is nothing other than the in-breaking of Jesus Christ—sometimes hidden in the field, sometimes as a book thrown at Mrs. Turpin's head,[7] but always as the surprising disruption of faith. Then, through faith, the goodness of the boundaries are more fully recognized, and new life springs forth. This is a joyful apocalypse; it is new creation, always new beginnings.

The new creation that the encounter actualizes, this new birth, is only known in life as dynamic, continual new beginnings. In this life, I am still a concupiscent being. My desires (both physical and spiritual) are turned in on myself. I am still in this world that does not want new creation; in fact, I will even resist it. But the amazing gift is that participation in God's new creation, these continually new beginnings offered to each of us, is always sanctified beginnings,[8] or holy beginnings. New beginnings are always held in and by God. New creation is God's work, and only God's work. The Holy Spirit never tires of starting afresh, each day, with every person. This new creation is known in faith, as faith, through faith, with faith. I only see it dimly as in a vision; it is the hidden way of the Spirit.

This faith, Luther writes, "is a sort of knowledge or darkness that nothing can see. Yet the Christ of whom faith takes hold is sitting in this darkness as God sat in the midst of darkness on Sinai and in the temple. Therefore our 'formal righteousness' . . . is faith itself, a cloud in our hearts, that is, trust in a thing we do not see, in Christ, who is present especially when he cannot be seen."[9] This faith is a sort of knowledge that is contrary to all knowledge; it is not rational or cognitive; it is, according to Luther, "a sort of knowledge or darkness that nothing can see";[10] it is directing a community to that which is hidden way, to the originary history, to that singular event that continually resonates throughout the community's witness and in each life.

This is the faith lived in community. It was received in the community, in the worshipping community around word and sacrament. Perhaps a person may receive this faith in many other moments as well, but one place where I am assured the Holy Spirit is present is within the community, in the communion of saints, as the community listens, washes, eats, shares, confesses, prays, gives thanks, sings, and bears the burdens of each other. These simple rituals of the praying community hold the inaccessible, the hidden, allowing it to continually return within the community, shaping its faith. Perhaps they are a bit like that darkness or cloud that is difficult to define. Therefore, realities such as tasting and seeing are so critical to the experience of faith. Faith is beyond the cognitive, deeper than the emotional. It holds these two together, a sweetness that can be tasted, a beauty that can be seen.

Faith is experienced in the community. It is the ground from which many gifts of the Spirit spring forth: love, joy, peace, forbearance, kindness, goodness, faithfulness, gentleness, and self-control (Gal 5:22–23). As complete trust in God, in the midst of darkness, it sweeps the community and each person in a new orientation, as new creation. Judgment is left behind, and life becomes a call to reconciliation, within each person, within the community, and with the world.

This gift of reconciliation—reconciled with God and with one another—does not immediately create a bed of roses. It implies a struggle. (More on this struggle in Chapter 4.) The hidden way is not always what I expect or want. Things happen. Things happen that I don't want to happen. Unexpected things. I must be careful not to confuse each and every event of happening with that hidden way or as a sign from God. East interpretations can disturb and easily distract me from the course. Discernment is required. The hidden way, God's path of reconciliation, though, always will be for the building up of community; it will be rooted in God's immeasurable goodness, in silence, even when tempests roar. Selah. This reconciliation permeates all aspects of dying and living. It weaves a path through many resistances.

Luther, when writing about the way on which faith leads, points out that suffering often is encountered. This suffering is not inherent to the way. It arises from the incomprehension of the world, the inability of others to see the hidden way. It arises from my own inability—psychologically, mentally, intellectually, physically, emotionally—to see the way in which the Spirit is leading.

> The hidden way, God's path of reconciliation, though, always will be for the building up of community.

Luther puts it this way: "For whoever has faith, trusts in God, and shows love to his neighbor, practicing it day by day, must needs suffer persecution. . . . Thus faith, by much affliction and persecution, ever increases, and is strengthened day by day. A heart thus blessed with virtues never can rest or restrain itself, but rather pours itself out again for the benefit and service of the [neighbor], just as God has done to it."[11] In the midst of suffering, in the midst of assaults or persecutions (of all types, both inner and outer), the community can sing, if only a song of lament. At other times, the heart sings without restraint, giving of itself to the other.

Faith cannot rest or restrain itself. It gives of itself and sets me off on a journey that is a joyful, simple, merciful obedience—for it is in this obedience of faith that I discover the treasure in the field, that I delight in God's law, that I taste God's word, which is finer than sweet wine. This obedience defines life, the boundaries of the field. Luther says, "For faith is nothing else than obedience to the Spirit. But there are different degrees of obedience to the Spirit. For one [person] is obedient and believes in this respect, and another [person] in another respect, and yet all of us are in the one faith."[12]

The forgiveness of sins, that act of reconciliation on God's part by which a person is freed of all burdens, is the source of this joy-filled gushing over into good works, of a life immersed in practice, in discipleship; in short, a spiritual life in which we "call upon God, give thanks to God, preach God, praise and confess God. [We] do good to [our] neighbor, and serve [our neighbor]; do [our] duty. These are truly good works, which flow from this faith and joy conceived in the heart because we have the forgiveness of sins freely through Christ," as Luther puts it.[13]

Discipleship flows from justification. God does not want sacrifice—that is, a required or mandated discipleship or obedience—but an obedience from faith alone. Discipleship is the umbrella under which all spiritual practices, all spiritual disciplines, are located. Spiritual discipline is not striving toward an ideal, toward a state of being, nor even toward a goal. It is following and continually conforming to the one being followed. Jesus's call is both death and life. Jesus calls each one in the midst of their life situation, and in that call faith is created, called forth, and engaged. This call that awakens faith is a call into community. Spiritual discipline, then, is following, participating in God's work of continual new beginnings in and through this unique community, through this mystery of communion. Discipleship and participation are joy and thanksgiving.

Bonhoeffer links discipleship and baptism. This can be surprising if discipleship is considered a condition of baptism rather than a sweet fruit of it. It also can be surprising if baptism is relegated to a one-time event in the past, as a mere rite of initiation. Bonhoeffer, however, points out that to speak about discipleship, Paul, particularly in the letter to the Romans, speaks about baptism. Discipleship and baptism are two expressions for one reality: the gospel operative in life. This link is crucial, for it highlights a fundamental characteristic of the journey: it is a baptismal journey. Or as Luther puts it, all of life is a spiritual baptism.[14] A baptismal spirituality emerges, defining life according to faith and the hidden way the Holy Spirit inserts the seeking person into God's plan—that is, into conformity with Jesus Christ.

A Spiritual Discipline

In the churches and streets of Leipzig, continual new beginnings occurred through a simple repeated communal and liturgical event. A communal and public prayer occasioned this new beginning. This prayer provided a room, a welcome, a forum, an unexpected place where a particular ritual pattern opened up toward disruption. The communal prayer offered a space where believers could rehearse and improvise a new identity. This improvisation (and sustained rehearsal) involved a continual undressing—that is, the identity that their culture and their political system provided, the identity that even to some degree the church provided, was questioned. They questioned this given identity using the words, the language, they had received in prayer as they sang and listened and read and reflected together.

Improvisation was a key characteristic of this new identity. But every good improvisation builds on a structure, a form; it is based on a musical scale. These young people and their pastors delved into what the tradition gave them (communal prayer, for example), and they adapted the pattern to their specific, often crisis-filled, situation. Many times, they did not know what they were doing. Often, it was poorly improvised.[15] No matter how the improvisation happened, they engaged a form of prayer rather than dismissing it completely. Of course, this meant that at times, as Pastor Groeger noted, the prayers "were all over the map. Prayers shouldn't be just a sermon, but this happened over and over again. Of course, the problem was that these prayers were also the only form that people had to express their views, opinions." The gathering for communal prayer was liberating for a walled-in society. The petitions within the prayer invited the community into a communion beyond their immediate boundaries, beyond the political walls that fenced them in.

> The gathering for communal prayer was liberating for a walled-in society.

In its most basic form, communal prayer consists of psalmody and intercessory prayer or petition (more on this in Chapters 5–6). Singing and meditating on the Psalms constitutes in itself the proclamation of the word. This singing, often followed by a Scripture reading and then by intense prayer for the needs of the world, opens up the gathered assembly to the outside world. In many of the prayers in East Germany, the emphasis was placed on the petitions, on intercessory prayer. Sometimes the petitions became merely a description of the problems the world and the people confronted, or, as mentioned, they became mini-sermons. The pastors and lay leaders sought to refocus the prayers not simply around petitions but also around praise and thanksgiving. Pastor Groeger noted the importance for them of Luther's definition of prayer in his early commentary on the Lord's Prayer (1519): praising God, thanksgiving, and petition.

The prayers of the numerous small groups varied from place to place, but generally consisted in a simple pattern. (The prayers of the larger gatherings in summer and fall 1989 had their own specific pattern.) The prayers began with songs from around the world; South African freedom songs, African American spirituals, and many Taizé songs (many of the traditional hymns were not as important). Songs were sung throughout the prayer, and were often the same from week to week, to help all those participate who were seeking but not yet versed in the songs of faith. Psalms were an important part of the prayer, especially Psalm 85. Scripture was read. Particular texts held a prominent place, such as the Sermon on the Mount, the visions in Isaiah (swords to plowshares), Revelation (making everything new), and Exodus (being on the move). Announcements were important in order to know what was happening around them, especially any news about friends or acquaintances who may have been stopped or interrogated. Guitarists played a critical, almost presiding role.

Occasionally, there was a short homily, then came the petitions, which presented the complexities of their situation and the situation of the world. In some cases, candles were lighted at the end of the prayer.

As people struggled to live into and transform this simple pattern, bringing it into dialogue with the reality of their lives, communal, public prayer became something of an unexpected baptismal improvisation or discipline.[16] They did not know what would happen or what would be said (during the petitions, for example, or sometimes during the time for announcements). Listening to the voices of those present became a discipline in itself—listening and then carrying the concerns in prayer and song.

Through communal prayer, they lived something like a baptismal discipline. Bonhoeffer does not write specifically about a baptismal discipline, but he does write about a secret discipline alive within the gathered assembly. How this secret discipline is defined remains a subject of debate, but I propose that it is closely related to baptism. In baptism, as Bonhoeffer points out, a person has made a break from the world, and this break is absolute.[17] But this break has nothing esoteric about it. The baptized person is not initiated into a secret society. The church does not separate itself from the world as a type of utopian society. Rather, the break that occurs in baptism immediately pushes one back into the world. The baptized person becomes part of a community that receives the cross as gift—that is, the suffering of the world as responsibility. A community is formed that follows Jesus publicly and belongs to the world.[18]

In Luther's enumeration of the marks of the church (see Chapter 2), the seventh is the holy possession of the cross. There are not many societies that promise their new recruits a cross. There are not many groups, Luther writes, that are asked to "endure every misfortune and persecution . . . inward sadness, timidity, fear, outward poverty, contempt, illness, and weakness, in order to become like their head, Christ."[19] This suffering—and here is the main point—is not just personal misfortune or suffering that befalls an individual in life; it is a public suffering because of one's adherence to the word of God, because of one's obedience to this hidden way that the Holy Spirit is tracing, a way that contradicts the values, goals, and privileges of society. Struggle accompanies faith.

Bonhoeffer can call this public discipline of the community secret because the world does not recognize the source of the discipline: the cross. Christians are in the world but not *of* the world. The world does not recognize the marks and power of the cross living in the community. The world is looking for possessions, whereas this community is literally possessed. Often, the community of the faithful is labeled as weak, powerless, insignificant, pacifist, perhaps even unpatriotic. No one, for example, cared about or paid attention to the small prayer groups gathering in East Germany during the 1950s, '60s, '70s, and '80s. The immediate and obvious explanation of the fall of the Berlin Wall, according to more sophisticated Western intelligence, was American military superiority. The witness to the gospel is unrecognized.

This hidden or secret discipline, however, is not a reclusive discipline. In *Letters and Papers from Prison*, Bonhoeffer states that the discipline of the Christian life is "living unreservedly in life's duties, problems, successes and failures, experiences and perplexities. In so doing we throw ourselves completely into the arms of God, taking seriously not our own sufferings, but those of God in the world."[20] Here is another description of that beautiful field described in Psalm 16: each person is completely in the arms of God and bearing, with God, the suffering of the world. Baptism pulls the community out of the world to throw it back into the world in order to find God suffering in the neighbor and in those who are unrecognized by the world. Baptism understood as communion in the suffering and death of Christ also means a communion in the suffering and death of the world, the neighbor. Though baptism may be described as a secret discipline, it is very public.

Communal prayer as a manifestation of spiritual discipline has led to an unexpected place: the baptismal font. It has led to a place of immersion, of dying and new creation. Baptism frames the deep reality of life: that a person dies with Jesus to be raised with Jesus, to die with God and to be raised with God, to be liberated from the oppression of self-constructed identities, and to be sent off on a journey ever deeper into righteousness, shaped by the Holy Spirit into God's unique and merciful imagination for every person.

For Luther, though baptism happens only once in a person's life, its significance encompasses all of life. Baptism is an ongoing exercise, a discipline that is engaged in the midst of the struggles of life. Every death I die—the little deaths of everyday living and of life's bigger struggles—all of these deaths train, form, prepare, and conform me to Christ. The limits, boundaries, and constraints, the many deaths I experience, make me more deeply aware of the context of my life. In this perspective, the reality of my neighbor, both in their suffering and joy, which I also experience, outlines the boundaries of my life and of the community's life. The world is never absent; it is an ever-present reality into which baptism immerses the community.

> Engaging in communal prayer, as these young Christians did in the former East Germany, was a visible manifestation of their baptismal vocation.

Engaging in communal prayer, as these young Christians did in the former East Germany, was a visible manifestation of their baptismal vocation. The world did not recognize it, and perhaps these young people didn't recognize it either, but through that adventure in prayer, the Holy Spirit continued to trace its way of peace. The young (and not so young) people participating in the prayer groups witnessed to this life of the Spirit that, in the most unassuming ways, continually makes things new.

Luther, in the preface to the *Large Catechism*, defines such prayer:

Nothing is so powerfully effective against the devil, the world, the flesh, and all evil thoughts as to occupy one's self with God's word, to speak about it and meditate upon it, in the way that Psalm 1:2 calls those blessed who "meditate on God's law day and night." Without doubt, you will offer up no more powerful incense or savor against the devil than to occupy yourself with God's commandments and words and to speak, sing, or think about them. Indeed, this is the true holy water and sign that drives away the devil and puts him to flight.[21]

The definition of prayer here is large: it is meditation on the word; it is occupying oneself with the commandments, speaking, singing, and thinking about them. Prayer is not only an individual activity but something that happens "together." It is a communal activity, as Luther notes. "What matters is not the places and buildings where we assemble, but this unconquerable prayer alone, and our really praying it together and offering it to God."[22] When, in the early years of the Reformation, the daily mass was eliminated, Luther did not eliminate regular communal prayer.[23] Luther replaced the daily mass with communal and public prayer, primarily matins and vespers (morning and evening prayer).[24] There is little doubt, for Luther, about the necessity of a regular practice of prayer, both communal and individual.[25]

Luther describes daily prayer as a baptismal reality. Daily prayer—this *holy water and sign*—drives the devil away, drives the darkness away, breaks the gates of hell, and opens the gates of trust. Prayer is a practice of baptism. It is not a second baptism but "almost like a baptism."[26] Prayer is both rupture and displacement, where new beginnings and life, new creation, continually return to become embodied in life. Such prayer, communal and individual, exercises the community in its identity as a baptized people, and embodies that baptism in resistance and struggle against all oppressive, enslaving powers and principalities that confront people anew every day.

Prayer defeats the devil, Luther says. Following the example of communal prayer in East Germany, this prayer defeats evil in all of its many manifestations. Communal public prayer defeated the oppressive, stifling, despotic regimes in Eastern Europe. And Luther calls—though more importantly, baptism calls—to this continual practice of daily prayer in society today for spiritual renewal and nourishment, yes, but more as witness to the cross present in many places today.

Prayer is not a ladder leading upward toward a distant God or toward simply finding some form of spiritual balance in life. Rather, as both Luther and Bonhoeffer point out, it is a daily dying and rising. Such prayer, when practiced in community, can be a risky business. It states: something is more important than just *my* individual salvation. An ardent prayer for peace in the world is more urgent than my personal well-being. Justice, in fact, is more important. The coming kingdom of God in peace and righteousness is more important. The focus is continually on the other, on the neighbor, on the world.

Without realizing it, perhaps, communal prayer in East Germany became for those involved, and for the church, a form of resistance, even if that had not been their intention. Initially, as Pastor Groeger described it, "The young people had an incredible fear of nuclear weapons and the continual buildup of nuclear arms along the East-West border. The official church said first of all that the matter of peace was not 'our' topic (that is, it was a political topic), but then it became clear that for the young people, it was 'our' topic; it was all about peace, prayers for peace."[27] In this prayer for peace, their fear was transformed into a gospel plea. And the world was at the center of this plea.

Prayer is passive resistance: the precariousness of a lighted candle facing communist soldiers in 1989. Prayer is a continual confrontation, an exercise of the powerlessness of baptism and an unexpected disruption of the order of the world as the Holy Spirit permeates the cosmos and reclaims it.

Joyful Obedience

The example at the heart of this exploration of spirituality been the communal prayer under oppression. It already has revealed several characteristics of a spirituality rooted in the gospel, in justification by faith alone. The Spirit's work shapes this gospel spirituality. Let's look more closely at what Luther—a theologian, a monk, a professor, and then a husband and father—says about such an experience of prayer.

Luther's writing, whether in a letter to his barber, Peter, or in his major commentary on the Lord's Prayer in the *Large Catechism*, or in various sermons, treats prayer in both dimensions, communal and individual.

Luther begins very simply. He notes first of all that one is commanded to pray. In the preface to the Lord's Prayer in the

Large Catechism, Luther writes, "The first thing to know is this: It is our duty to pray because of God's command. For we heard in the second commandment, 'You are not to take God's name in vain.' Thereby we are required to praise the holy name and to pray or call upon it in every need. For calling upon it is nothing else than praying."[28]

This command to pray is found in the second commandment (keeping God's name holy). It is mirrored in the second petition of the Lord's Prayer—hallowed be your name—"in which faith desires that God's name, praise, and honor be glorified, and that God's name be called upon in every need."[29] In the *Small Catechism*, Luther explains it this way: "So you see that in this petition, we pray for exactly the same thing that God demands in the second commandment: that his name should not be taken in vain by swearing, cursing, deceiving, and so forth, but used rightly to the praise and glory of God." The first petition of the Lord's Prayer calls on God's name and pleads for the word to be among us. This is the most fundamental need: that God's word be among the community, for without the word all is lost. The second petition names the most fundamental practice of life, the most fundamental expression of faith: calling on God's name.

However, this commandment to pray can quickly become itself a law, for I cannot always fulfill it as I should (or as I would like to) when I do not know what or how to pray. This is like a death. My heart is empty. I cannot believe or act as I should, and now I cannot even pray. I cannot keep God's word at the center. After an initial energized and hopeful start to a new spiritual practice, I quickly slack off or get bored. I'm not faithful to any sustained spiritual discipline. Too quickly, my best intentions evaporate. If it were up to me relying on my own heart or desire to pray, prayer never truly would happen.

The death of any ability to fulfill the commandments, or believe, or even pray—the death of even my affirmed spiritual gifts—seems preposterous to the old self that wants to cling to what I have in me. Yet, when Luther states that everyone needs to be taught how to pray, he asserts that prayer is not natural to human beings. In other words, human beings are not by nature praying creatures, though everyone might assume they are.[30] Bonhoeffer notes that human beings too often confuse "wishing, hoping, sighing, lamenting, rejoicing—all of which the heart can do on its own—with praying."[31] I confuse my spiritual desire or spiritual concupiscence with the work of the Holy Spirit. My spiritual desire seeks satisfaction, fulfillment, harmony, a balanced inner life, and it believes that it can achieve it through certain practices. But my prayer remains self-centered.

Praying is not just pouring out one's heart, for what does one do when, as Bonhoeffer asks, the heart is empty? Or when one feels nothing? Or when one feels totally abandoned? Prayer exists on another level of existence: in prayer, the Holy Spirit takes my emotions, my thoughts, even my body, and broadens and deepens them all, holding them and opening them to dimensions of God's righteousness, mercy, and immeasurable goodness, which I could not begin to imagine. The Holy Spirit imparts all aspects of my existence with an intensity that reveals a new horizon, a new way, and with this intensification, new affections.[32] New creation. I have a glimmer of this movement when listening to Bach's "St. Matthew's Passion" or Messiaen's "Quartet for the End of Time": a horizon spans out beyond the usual markers that I have crafted for my life and pushes me to see the expansive yet hidden markers God has established.[33]

This is the Holy Spirit's work, which is why Luther states that Christ himself teaches us how to pray: "That we may know what and how to pray, however, our Lord Christ himself has taught us both the way and the words, as we shall see."[34] God teaches us how to pray. God actually gives the words for prayer, deep within each heart.

> God teaches us how to pray. God actually gives the words for prayer, deep within each heart.

For Luther, prayer is pleading with God out of deep need, out of a great emptiness, a recognition of inability. Prayer is "drumming into God's ear" my very existence when the heart is full (of joy or pain) and when the heart is empty. The surprising, if not amazing, discovery is that this drumming and this pleading are not human works. The recognition of my need and the prayer that arises from this place of emptiness, need, despair, and tribulation is a work of the Holy Spirit, who continually "intercedes with sighs too deep for words" (Rom 8:26). This prayer—the words, voiced and voiceless of the Holy Spirit—is greater than one's heart, for it is grounded in God, who is always greater. "And by this we will know that we are from the truth and will reassure our hearts before [God] whenever our hearts condemn us; for God is greater than our hearts, and [God] knows everything" (1 John 3:19–20).

God knows each and every one and gives the words for prayer, particularly through the Lord's Prayer and the Psalms. Because I so easily can confuse a spiritual concupiscence with prayer, because I don't always distinguish between my own desire centered on myself and prayer, I am both commanded to pray and taught how to pray. The command to pray is something very different from a law that is imposed (though sometimes it also may be that). The command to pray establishes the heritage, that pleasant field, that God gives. The command is unlike anything you or I have received, for in this command God gives the very possibility of faith. "The reason [God] commands us to pray is so we will be filled with a sure and firm faith that we will be heard," Luther says.[35] The command reveals itself as promise.

Luther's affinity for Psalm 119 is comprehensible. Psalm 119 focuses on God's command as life-giving. God only commands what is life-giving. God's command is so intimately linked to God's promise that the two are one. The command takes away my reliance on all the reference points and crutches I have created for myself and gives me instead faith alone. The promise in the command? Here God listens. Here God is present. Obedience then springs forth joyfully, freely, spontaneously—an obedience that gathers the whole community together clandestinely and also sends it out into the streets, into an adventure in prayer.

Down to Earth

Prayer is not my work. It is not my action directed toward God. Prayer's source is always in Godself, in the Holy Spirit. Luther was very concerned that this question of directionality not be misdirected. Prayer is not just human words directed to God, nor human work attempting to reach God. Prayer is much more than an expression of desire.

Aspects of spirituality that Luther encountered in his day (still common today) place God up in the heavenly heights. The faithful ascend to God through diverse spiritual practices, such as silent meditation, communal worship, pilgrimages, fasting, works of justice, and so forth. The form of the practice is not as worrisome as the upward movement. In fact, Luther in his reform redefines this movement, this metaphorical conception of prayer.

What did this metaphor of prayer look like? It probably looks familiar. I have already described it several times in this brief writing: desire for God is at the heart of meditation, and meditation itself is focused on channeling that desire toward a union with God. Luther knew a practice that predated him: *lectio divina*. Briefly summarized, there are four elements to this pattern. The first, *lectio* (reading), is the careful repetition, recitation, of a short text of Scripture, either alone or in a group. This reading leads to the second stage: *meditatio* (meditation). *Meditatio* is a flight into the depth of the text (and of one's soul) in order to find the spiritual meaning or the inner message of the text. The third stage, *oratio* (prayer), is the personal response to the spiritual meaning discovered in the text, asking for the grace of the text to be true in one's own life, beseeching that one's life be lived in that truth. *Oratio* seeks to make the text's spiritual meaning personally relevant in one's own life. Finally, having accomplished these three stages, the pray-er reaches *contemplatio* (contemplation) or *illuminatio* (illumination).

Contemplation is a vision of the mystery that is God. In contemplation, the pray-er has reached the highest expression of love for God. The defining characteristic of the ascent is love. The one who loves more and more reaches the level of contemplation, the summit of love. That person has channeled all desire into this one great, silent act of love for God. Of course, in this paradigm for prayer, God also has granted grace (infused grace) along the way to help bring the pray-er to this level. The pray-er has been raised above meditation to experience a communion with God, an illumination in which God is seen. The Holy Spirit accomplishes this for dedicated pray-ers, allowing them to come into experiential contact with the one behind and beyond the text. Illumination is exposure to the divine presence, to God's truth and benevolence.

The experience of this schema of prayer is a movement upward from the text (from Scripture) toward contemplation, toward an illumination, quite literally seeing God through love, and experiencing communion with God. But Luther notices that in this progression, there is actually a movement not only behind the text but beyond it as well. The biblical text becomes vulnerable, he notes, to the whims of personal interpretation. Scripture may then be used to support a particular cause or interest, whether personal, of a special-interest group, or even in service to a national myth.[36] Everyone can find the meanings they imagine within the text, most through allegory (assigning contemporary meanings to persons, things, or events in a given text).

For Luther, however, the meaning of a scriptural text, which the Holy Spirit alone knows and imparts, the *mysteria*, or hidden meaning, is very different from what often is called the spiritual meaning.[37] Once again, the word *spiritual* creates some confusion; it can be understood in several ways. It is necessary, then, to turn to theological grammar to parse out this confusion. The challenge remains the same: drawing the distinction between that which is of the Holy Spirit and of the human spirit.

Luther's theological grammar radically disrupts the traditional metaphor of ascending prayer. As is so often the case in Luther's reforming activity, though, he does not throw everything out but instead seeks to reconfigure or rewrite prayer in light of justification by faith alone, reinterpreting a spiritual practice so that the gospel can be more clearly heard. In the case of *lectio divina*, Luther does not discard it as a practice but rearranges it, making one radical replacement. The last step of *lectio divina*—contemplation or illumination—is replaced by *tentatio*, "temptation," or, in German, *Anfechtung*.

Luther's rewriting of *lectio divina* is found in the preface to his German works, written in 1539.[38] It serves here as an invaluable insight into how he understands not only prayer but theology: the work of the theologian is rooted in a simple tripartite pattern of prayer.

Luther's reform places *oratio* (prayer) at the beginning. In prayer, I bow, bend my knees, and express my indebtedness to God. I cannot start anything—any searching, any endeavor—without first asking that the Holy Spirit guide me and the community. Humility is the first characteristic of prayer. *Kyrie eleison.* This prayer, Luther notes, could be centered in Psalm 119, as it places the word of God front and center: a word to be praised, sought after, and lived out.

The second stage, *meditatio* (meditation), Luther fuses with *lectio* (reading). For him, these two are not separate activities. The pray-er does not move from a simple reading into the greater depths (or heights) of meditation. No, meditation is already the very physical act of reading. Holding these two activities together is critical for Luther, for it abets the tendency of the heart to go off searching for the spiritual (understood here as self-imagined or self-invented) meaning. In meditation, the pray-er is not seeking some secret code in the text but rather is listening intently to the text in its simple historical meaning. Luther writes, "Thus 'literal meaning' is not a good term, because Paul interprets the letter quite differently than they [Origen and company] do. Those who call it 'grammatical, historical meaning' do better."[39]

The letter and the literal are not to be equated. In other words, the literal meaning is not to be given ultimate value. Rather, the text is to be understood in its historical context and situation. The pray-er is to struggle even with the grammar of the text. Through this effort, the Holy Spirit then will reveal the hidden meaning, the true spiritual meaning, the *mysteria*—in other words, what this text reveals about God's promise, the gospel. The Holy Spirit will disclose "the hidden understanding about Christ."[40] The Holy Spirit reveals, hidden as it may be, that singular event, which continually delineates a way for the community.

The key characteristic of this second stage is that the reading and meditating, the historical and the spiritual, are not separated. God is always acting in history: the Holy Spirit is continually writing a history within history. Through meditation the pray-er is not taken out of history or inducted into new mysteries, nor are they inventing new meanings by which they could contain or control God. Rather, the one praying enters ever deeper into God's continual activity, the work of the Holy Spirit. This activity of the Holy Spirit, discerned in silence and through attentive listening, leads to the unexpected. Often this means that the text occasions a confrontation. The pray-er may dispute and argue with the words, Luther suggests. The text pushes back. This confrontation takes place not only in the study, as the pray-er meditates on the text with a Greek or Hebrew dictionary next to them, but also as they walk, meditate, speak, sing, hear, and read, by day and by night.[41]

> God always is acting in history: the Holy Spirit is continually writing a history within history.

This study and confrontation is not only a private affair conducted in the secret of my room; it is also a public affair. The activities of meditation that Luther names are also all communal liturgical activities, just as the marks of the church are all communal activities. Together a community speaks and sings and listens in a regular rhythm, from day to day, week to week, season to season, and it does so in a particular pattern. Meditation is not left to the whims of one's personal or private space. Meditation demands the external, the outer manifestation, a physical activity, the public exercise of reading and praying that always will involve others. These outward activities (preaching included), Luther writes, were not given in vain. Through them, the Holy Spirit continually pushes community (you and me) beyond itself and toward both God and neighbor.

But meditation is not the final step. There is one more surprising move: *tentatio, Anfechtung,* or temptation. Luther calls it the touchstone. The German word *Anfechtung* in Luther's use holds many layers of meaning. It is wrong to simply or solely translate it as "temptation." Luther uses another German word, *Versuchung* (literally, "temptation"), alongside *Anfechtung,* suggesting varied levels of signification.

In order to parse what this important word signifies for Luther, it is perhaps best to begin with the role of *Anfechtung* in the trilogy of prayer. First, the summit of prayer (illumination) in the classic pattern of *lectio divina* is upended and replaced by something that could be considered its opposite: temptation. Prayer is not leading the pray-er up to the heavenly heights; prayer is not helping them ascend to see God residing in full splendor on a throne. Rather, in prayer, the pray-er is confronted with the God of Scripture, with God in a manger and on a cross, with God in the midst of life. The incarnate God comes down and encounters you and me and the community here.

In prayer, I am not purifying desire in order to see God; I am not trying to perfect love within myself to be more like God. Instead, I am being disrupted in my life, in my context, and in that disruption, in the midst of that struggle, I discover God coming down. Prayer does not take me out of this world but throws me more fully back into it. Struggle is no stranger. Or, as Oswald Bayer puts it, "Whoever meditates, must suffer."[42] Prayer is not an escape but an embrace of all aspects of life, holding all the joys and sufferings, hope and anxieties, contentment and pain, together under God's word, under God's immeasurable mercy and love.

The direction of prayer is reversed. God comes to you and me and the community; the Holy Spirit molds the community according to God's word, and not without struggle. Not Christianity lite, made of people barely distinguishable from the rest of society, not a hermetically sealed community separated from the world, but a people of faith living in the midst of the world's struggles. Through prayer, through this experience of *tentatio* or *Anfechtung*, struggle and disruption, the walls of inner resistance are broken down. Faith redefines life, together with others. The boundaries that God establishes mark for the community and for each individual a wonderful space of freedom, but this adventure in prayer is never without a struggle and often comes with suffering. Freely, willingly, obediently, the community walks out spontaneously into the night, into the street with candles lighted to meet neighbors—and with them, in them, Jesus.

4

Baptismal Spirituality

Experientia

A theologian is made, Luther writes, not through "thinking, reading, and speculating" but through experience.[1] The mystery that is God is experienced, but not in just any experience. Theologians—and here the definition of theologian is broad and encompassing—are formed not simply through the study of books but through a particular form of experience. What type of experience? Luther provides further insight when he writes, "No university crowns anyone like this [as a true theologian], only the Holy Spirit."[2] The experience to which Luther refers has something to do with the Holy Spirit's work.

Knowledge is situated not in speculation but in experience.[3] Luther often uses the Latin word *experientia* to describe this phenomenon, even when writing in German. The story of the underground prayer groups in Leipzig provides a glimpse into experientia, discerning a hidden reality (God's presence and therefore action) in all the events of their lives, both in joy and in despair, both in hope and in suffering. Experientia defines a spiritual and a physical landscape. This chapter will look more closely at what it entails. I will use the Latin word to avoid any confusion with experience as it is usually understood—for example, when someone says, "Wow! What a great experience!" referring to a great vacation or adventure or other event.

This landscape is a place of struggle (*Anfechtung*) through all the ups and downs of living, and in that struggle a discovery is made: life is shaped by a singular event that resonates throughout time. Luther explains how life is shaped as he reflects on Paul's verse in Romans, "*Justus ex fide sua vivit.*" Luther writes, "The righteous [person] draws [their] life out of [their] faith, and faith is that whereby [they are] counted righteous before God [Rom 1:17]."[4] Life is engendered and held by faith. Faith as a gift reveals the boundaries, the beautiful field, the goodly heritage (Ps 16), the contours of life as God has determined. Within that field, God's way becomes known, not as a concept grasped cognitively, but as something tangible, audible, visible, palatable, and fragrant.

The discovery of life through faith, literally drawing life out of faith, is experientia. Through experientia faith becomes a historically lived reality. Experientia is like a continual training or exercise that enables me to see both the visible and the invisible, the Holy Spirit active in this history around me. This exercise employs all my emotions, senses, and intelligence; it is knowing of the heart.

In this life, faith constitutes my relationship to God. Experientia names the way in which faith affects me in everyday life (as a historical reality). It is a daily dying and rising with the one who has died and is alive. Experientia describes the confrontation, disruption, and deconstruction of identity and the advent of new creation—secret and barely visible, but drawing me always deeper into a life and identity I never could have constructed for myself.

Faith is a very different type of knowing. It establishes a theological grammar that distinguishes what is of God and what comes from human beings. As a distinction that

> Faith is a very different type of knowing.

must not be blurred, this theological grammar breaks down the towers human beings want to build. This grammar could be rightly described as traumatic for the self-centered, introspective inclination in each person. This grammar names that singular event that is Jesus Christ, which cuts through identities, cultures, societies, histories, and myths, through the heart and the world humans create around themselves. It points to that event that irrupts unexpectedly in the midst of the most banal activities of the day and in the fathomless pits of the night. The event that irrupts, that keeps returning, remains always outside my ability to control it or hem it in. A singular, traumatic event continually affects my life.

The inability to capture or to know this event in all its dimensions (and its corresponding responsibility) witnesses to a different type of existence. It traces a different history. The impossibility of encircling, systematizing, or representing the traumatic points *me* to a different type of knowing, one beyond the cognitive, rational appropriation of facts or empirical data. It points to the life and knowing of faith.

It is characteristic of faith not to know and yet to know in ways so intimate that words fail. How is this possible? The traumatic event "consists not only in having confronted death but in *having survived, precisely, without knowing it*," Cathy Caruth writes.[5] There is something in the experience, in the singular event that cannot be grasped by understanding and that widens the horizons set by the categories of rationality. Cognitive knowing is not able to capture this event and categorize it because trauma "does not simply serve as record of the past but precisely registers the force of an experience that is not yet fully owned."[6]

The Christ event is never fully owned by history. Faith as knowing, however, is a continual awakening to the event that was not fully understood, a continual "becoming for us" of the event.[7] Immediate understanding (knowing defined as immediate perception of the here and now) and even representational knowledge (that attempt to grasp and control a totality, as Michel de Certeau has shown)[8] are displaced in this assertion or shown to be incomplete. Rather, connection to the past, to history, and to the present is through a discernment of something latent, something unobservable, something that makes itself known, that surfaces in unexpected ways. Trauma—the Christ event—is latent in every moment, in every event. It hides and reveals God's hidden way, though always under guises, through contraries, even opposites. This is the way of the Spirit in the world, a history that the Spirit is writing through you and me and the community.

That which is latent is precisely that which was not known, not immediately perceived in the moment of the event. In his second Psalms commentary, Luther writes about this latency as an absence, one that is somehow "apprehended" but only by faith: *"Verba enim spiritus sunt annunciata de re absente et non apparente, per fidem apprehendenenda"* (The words of the Spirit announce an absent thing, not to be seen, but apprehended by faith).[9] The Spirit points to that which is latent in the event, the traumatic thread that constitutes history and that only faith discerns. Experientia is a continual living into that which is latent, absent to reason: a secret that is nonetheless for all the world.

This strange type of knowing that is faith displaces me as a subject. The categories of the cognitive, representational knowledge, which impose their own schema on the data of experience, are left behind. The knowing that is faith is more like entering into a powerlessness, living in an incompleteness without fear or desire—a possibility born out of God's reconciling act (God reconciled all to Godself). This knowing (grounded in reconciliation) is a mutual dependence on others, a bearing of others and being carried by them. This is the astounding feature of the hidden way: communion. The witnesses in East Germany have lived it; the way of the Spirit, a spiritual life, is not about me but for and with the other in an adventure only God can trace.

The treasure found in the field, Jesus Christ, is a treasure of mercy, immeasurable goodness, forgiveness, reconciliation, and new beginnings that defines all life and from which all of life is drawn out. When experientia is understood, as the field in which the Holy Spirit exercises the seeking one ever more deeply in faith, the radical move Luther accomplishes when he displaces illumination in favor of *tentatio* or *Anfechtung* becomes more accessible. Experientia is this displacement of illumination by *Anfechtung*, and it is good to spend some time with this displacement and dig deeper into the struggle that *Anfechtung* describes.

In the Psalms, as noted earlier, the heart of the saints is revealed. Their struggle and joys, their arguments with and against God, and their praise, resistance, and submission—handing all over to God—is shared. Through the words of their struggle and their joys recorded in the Psalms, the "finest example" Luther writes that the words of the psalms record the saints' struggle and joys. The psalms serve as the finest example for the reader, the pray-er, not only to see but to enter truly into their experientia.

What are these struggles at the heart of prayer? Perhaps the simplest manner to approach these questions is through the lens of the first commandment: you shall have no other gods. Faith is the subject of the first commandment, a trust poured out into hearts. When life is drawn from this faith, when life is meditating on God's law day and night, a way opens up, one new and totally unexpected. But when trust is placed in other things that are valued above God, competing gods are created,[10] and trust is continually diminished to the size of those gods. This is the opposite of faith. A trust misplaced, what Luther calls unbelief, shapes life, curving one in on oneself or on that small group that is valued. A trust misplaced closes spaces and attempts to create its own righteousness, its own justification, its own expression and identity. Faith, on the other hand, shapes life toward original righteousness, the beautiful field, the open spaces that God has established.

There is no middle road: faith in God or unbelief. Throughout his life, Luther comes back to this point in his ongoing commentary on Psalm 1. Already in the first Psalms commentary (1513–15), Luther defines the way of the sinner as the way of the godless. The foolish one, who does not rely on God's law, simply follows the trends of the

> Faith, on the other hand, shapes life toward original righteousness, the beautiful field, the open spaces that God has established.

time.[11] In the second commentary (1519–21), Luther sharpens his position. Not only is the distinction drawn between those who have faith in God (piety) and those who "think bad" about God (the godless), but these positions take root deep in their persons. Piety and godlessness are not just moral positions; they describe the very "source of morals" in the heart.[12] In other words, you and I draw out from this source (faith/piety or hatred of God) the very manner of living in the world.

Then later, in the 1540s, Luther insists even more adamantly on the distinction. The godless are those who mix up or blur the distinction between what is human and what is of God.[13] They like to make what is theirs into something godly, endowing it with divine or holy traits. In other words, for those who believe, God is simply an object to put into their lives like a puzzle piece. Rather than the one who alone is, God becomes simply part of their identity, part of their life. Their own identity and context remain front and center.

This situation is encouraged by the evil one (or, to employ Luther's personification, devil or Satan—terms I will use interchangeably), who, Luther contends, is a master of mixing up the two realms: that which is God's and that which is human.[14] The evil one likes to get people entangled in that blurred vision as well. There is nothing he likes better than when I think I'm doing God's work but I'm actually just serving myself. And for those in whom the Holy Spirit is awakening, nurturing, and increasing faith, whose lives are being drawn from faith, the devil is quick to intervene. Here is the beginning of *Anfechtung* (temptation), a major part of experientia. Besides temptation, other words describe this phenomenon: struggle, trial, affliction, confrontation, and disruption.

Struggle

The beginnings, growth, and strengthening of faith are resisted at every occasion by the evil one, who wants me to always turn toward myself and not trust God alone. This intervention is experienced as struggle. Of course, the evil one is not interested in the person who simply has a narrative faith. Knowing

Scripture is important, but the evil one knows it too and yet does not encounter Christ.[15] However, the evil one becomes more concerned when someone moves from merely knowing the story to actually encountering God's word for them (the "for you" of the gospel). The evil one wants to prevent that encounter, that growth of faith.

As mentioned earlier, my old nature, my curved-in-upon-myself existence, the old Adam and Eve, helped along by the evil one, is always busy resisting the Spirit's work. Though the old has been drowned in baptism, it is a surprisingly good swimmer, Luther notes. The evil one, the force that works against those following Christ, is constantly attempting to maintain the status quo, continually focusing their energies on themselves and away from Christ.

Luther, when writing about the general prayer or common prayer (what some call today the universal prayer or the prayer of the people in Sunday worship), notes that the devil always resists prayer. "The devil . . . does all that he can to prevent such prayer. This is why he lets us build handsome churches, endow many colleges, make anthems, read and sing, celebrate many masses, and multiply ceremonies beyond all measure. This brings him no sorrow. On the contrary, he helps us to do it, so that we will regard such ways the best and think that in doing them we have done our whole duty."[16]

The devil doesn't want the faith community engaging an intense prayer toward God and for the neighbor, because he knows in such prayer the Holy Spirit exercises faith. He wishes to distract the community from such a prayer. Temptation, in this case, is simply slipping back into the monotone, into the way things have always been. Curiously, speaking of the devil may conjure images of a red-horned creature enticing persons into nefarious activities, rather than his power to even more busily keep everything ordinary. Building churches, composing anthems, reading, and singing do not seem like activities of the evil one. Yet, Luther warns, the evil one can use such "good" activities to distract from the hidden way, from faith, from praising God, and from our responsibility to the neighbor.

When the evil one sees that the Spirit is killing the self-constructed, buffered, self-centered self, he resists. Satan desires that human beings live in an imagined self, in a glorified, spiritualized self that seeks God up in heaven. Satan wants the ego to reign. He wants to distract me and the community from the work that flows unrestrained from faith—namely, service of the neighbor, and creating with God a trustworthy world.[17] Temptation may be nothing else than slipping back into the way things have always been done. Temptation may also be a dismissal of God, an avoidance of the disruptive.

Struggle is my reaction to the disruptive work of the Holy Spirit. Rather than leading me up to the heavenly heights or helping me leave behind my experience, my heart, and my body, prayer brings me back to these things but prayer is now understood as the place where God encounters me and the community. God encounters the world here and now, not in an imagined heaven. Here and now, God encounters human beings, and through the Spirit begins the work of conforming them to Jesus

Christ. Here and now, the Spirit is continually creating, and Satan is continually resisting.

For Luther, this *tentatio—Anfechtung*—struggle expresses the force of an encounter, of a disruption. The encounter with the word of God is a confrontation. This encounter happens not only in the head but also in the body, in my whole being, my heart. In this encounter, I don't bring the word into me, where I can mull it over and discover its hidden meanings for my life, making it my own. No, the word I encounter in prayer calls me out of my sheltered identities, which I fabricate in a dance with culture, wealth, moral codes, ethnic codes, national myths, and everything else that creates a worldview. When the word calls me outward, I discover faith not as sacrifice but as a simple obedience to the way of the Spirit. I am slowly, day by day, conformed to Christ, made into a little Christ, made holy.

> Struggle is my reaction to the disruptive work of the Holy Spirit.

I'm linking *tentatio* and disruption. *Disruption* names a reality of prayer. In prayer, the usual references of faith that I have relied on are often taken away, even those reference points that have been anchors from early on in my faith life. The Spirit can take them all away. This is on some level quite disturbing: what the Holy Spirit had first given to sustain me on this journey—perhaps people or a place (such as camp or someone's welcoming home), a Scripture passage, or a piece of music or art—is taken away or not as accessible anymore. I find myself in a desert. God's word has disrupted the self, the context, and not only the life I have constructed but one that the Spirit itself has nurtured.

Prayer is confrontation with Scripture, with event, with people, with place, and all of these are latent with something from God. The Holy Spirit works through all of these and in even more ways. A surprising discovery is made in this confrontation with that latent something, with that which I cannot capture or control. I am actually freed from the burden of my ego, freed of my inclinations toward my own desire for fulfillment, my own reason, my own imagination, my own theories and interpretations. The burden of the self is taken off my shoulder. Here— experientia—I experience the sweetness and comfort of God's word, whose yoke is easy and whose burden is light (Matt 11:30). Yes, this gospel disruption is sweet, loving, mighty, and comforting because in that death I am reborn.[18]

Remember where this sweetness is experienced. It is not in the heights of illumination; it is not in the summit of human wisdom; it is not at the top of the ladder. The sweetness of the word is experienced here in the messiness of life, as I am confronted by a Scripture text, by that which I cannot control, by that which leaves me naked, by the Holy Spirit working through history in ways I cannot fully understand.

In the confrontation and the sweetness, in the disruption of all my desires—even my desire for God—God is creating something new. God is giving new life, sweeping you and me and the community up in new creation. In that disruption, God gives new birth. The emphasis here is on "God gives": I cannot grab this new life; I cannot create it for myself through deep centering;

I cannot control it or force the experience on myself (or on others). I only can be obedient to that disruption. Here is precisely where Satan intervenes. Satan wants to prevent that holy disruption and that obedience. Satan wishes that I step outside the field that is faith: "And you will be like God" (Gen 3:5). Satan wants to keep everyone in the realm of their desires, their needs, their longings, and their wishes, convincing them that they are holy and truly all that is needed to reach God. Satan relishes being in such spiritual concupiscence.

The problem, of course, is that my desires, my needs, my longings, and my wishes envision only a limited God, a god who will be there just for me, to make me happy, to make me feel fulfilled. The God I desire looks a lot like myself and the world as I conceive of it. That is also one of the dangers of the *imitatio Christi*: the Christ I wish to imitate risks becoming the Christ of my imagination, the Christ of my culture and race and gender. *Imitation* is a limited word. When I imitate something, the focus of action remains on me: How well am I doing what Jesus did? I remain the subject of the action. *Imitatio* is a feeble attempt at self-fulfillment. On the contrary, with the notion of *conformitas*, God is the one working through the word, working through experientia, acting on me, continually making me and the community holy. *Conformitas* is God's work—a disruptive, creative, revealing, life-giving work.

> The God I desire looks a lot like myself and the world as I conceive of it.

A spiritual journey engages you and me and the community on this hidden way that God traces—not toward an imagined happiness or stability, but concretely, experientially, into the struggles of life, of our neighbor, of the world. The culmination of prayer is not up in the heavens, but following God into the anguish and struggle of this world. In that disruption and obedience, faith encompasses my life, touching all those places of suffering and anguish, joy and contentment, and I experience what Psalm 1 implies when it begins, "Happy are those . . ." Fulfillment or wholeness now takes on a very different meaning. It is known in the most incomplete and broken aspects of life. It is known as the community, and each one of us waits vigilantly, patiently, silently. Fulfillment is not given in the ways of the world; rather, God makes every person holy. Desire is replaced by faith. This spiritual journey is a unique baptismal discipline.

Radical Reorientation

As I have shown, Luther disrupts the idea of prayer as an ascent. Prayer is not an ascent that continually purifies the person of everything physical, raising them up above the material messiness of life in order to contemplate God. Prayer as ascent is not a foreign concept. It is operative in churches and in many spiritual movements. It is operative wherever "God" is placed in one realm and the human community is placed in another. It is operative wherever anything of God's realm is called sacred and anything in this world is called secular—or any other such nominal distinctions. It is operative in a theology that reveres the sacraments as a type of ladder from this world into God's reality, or that imagines God's grace to be some type of substance that gets channeled down to the worshipping community. It is equally operative in the most fundamentalist theologies that revere the law as a ladder to God.

Luther disrupts all these notions. But because he has destroyed these approaches (whether of purification and ascent or channeling), how does he speak about God's action in the world and the community's participation in that action? When Luther disrupts the common metaphor of ascent, with what does he replace it?

Luther works this out in his rewriting of the significance of the sacraments. Luther's struggle to find a language for faith, for experientia, for reception and obedience, is witnessed in his early sermons on the sacraments.[19] He finds the beginnings of a new language in rereading what the sacraments signify in daily lives.[20] This begins with the sacrament of baptism.

This metaphorical reframing has already been explored in the work of the Holy Spirit through prayer. Prayer is a confrontation, a struggle, and in that struggle or disruption (*tentatio*) of prayer, the Holy Spirit moves the pray-er to a new place. This confrontation, however, has already begun in the sacrament of baptism. At the beginning of a Christian life is this surprise—at least according to one metaphor—death. The baptized die with Christ to be raised with Christ. This metaphor predates Luther, of course. It is found in Paul's Letter to the Romans:

Do you not know that all of us who have been baptized into Christ Jesus were baptized into his death? Therefore we have been buried with him by baptism into death, so that, just as Christ was raised from the dead by the glory of the Father, so we too might walk in newness of life.

For if we have been united with him in a death like his, we will certainly be united with him in a resurrection like his. We know that our old self was crucified with him so that the body of sin might be destroyed, and we might no longer be enslaved to sin. For whoever has died is freed from sin. But if we have died with Christ, we believe that we will also live with him. (Rom 6:3–8)

This metaphor of dying and rising with Christ finds explicit liturgical expression in the early church. One example from the fourth-century church in Jerusalem is particularly pertinent. Cyril of Jerusalem is writing to those who have just been baptized and have communed in the Easter Vigil. Now they require further catechesis: they are introduced to the meaning of what they experienced in the sacraments. This teaching or instruction of the mystery is called mystagogy.

In the *Mystagogical Catechesis*, Cyril writes concerning baptism: "O surpassing loving-kindness! Christ received the nails in his undefiled hands and feet, and endured anguish; while to me, without suffering and toil, by the fellowship of his pain he [grants] salvation."[21] One phrase in particular stands out: "the fellowship of his pain." I, as an individual, have received salvation, but it is in the fellowship of Christ's pain. The first thing to be noted is that baptism is both an individual and a communal regeneration. When I enter the waters—whether as an adult or as a child—I enter a fellowship, specifically into the fellowship of Christ's pain, of Christ's suffering and death. How is this accomplished? Is it by imagining, in my spiritual practice, Christ's pain on the cross? Is it by trying to relive that pain through a film, for example? Is it by imitating that pain by inflicting pain on myself through ascetic practices or other imagined sufferings? Is it suffering an abusive relationship, thinking that thereby I imitate Christ's sacrifice? Or is it simply imposing a spiritual discipline on myself? No! So, how is this fellowship with Christ's suffering realized in me? By a fellowship in Christ's suffering, which is everywhere around me. In such a fellowship, I know salvation. But I'm jumping ahead. Let's get back to Cyril.

Cyril further emphasizes a critical and distinguishing characteristic of this fellowship as he writes, "Baptism is not just for the remission of sins. John's baptism conferred only the remission of sins. But baptism into Christ is, as Paul writes, 'a baptism into Christ's death.' It is a 'communion with Christ's true sufferings.'"[22] Once again, this communion with Christ's sufferings does not mean going to a movie such as *The Passion of the Christ*. Rather, it means picking up the cross that is discovered or heard in one's own life: not the cross that I have chosen but the cross that encounters me in the midst of life. It means listening and responding to the voice of the needy one, the suffering one who cries out to me. "See, this is my body," Jesus says.

There are many metaphors for baptism, but I'm focusing on only one for the moment: the tomb metaphor. The metaphors have varied because of cultural, historical contexts and perhaps because of the different spiritual needs of believers.[23] Other metaphors include (1) regeneration: the baptized are washed clean in the water of their past and are now made clean, new creations in Christ; (2) the font as a womb, closely linked to regeneration, but much more radically to baptism as new birth, being born again (for example, Nicodemus's encounter with Jesus in John 3); (3) water as source of life—the baptized are like trees that have their roots in the springs of living water or like branches grafted onto the tree of life that is Jesus Christ; and (4) new garment—the baptized are clothed in Jesus Christ.

Luther uses all of these metaphors, though the metaphor that dominates his thinking on baptism is dying and rising with Jesus. Let's look closer at what he says about the metaphor in order to clarify how he understands Paul's insistence on this unity (communion) that occurs in death and in resurrection, and what is meant by conformity to Jesus Christ. In the *Large Catechism*, Luther writes, "In baptism, every Christian has enough to study and practice all his or her life. Christians always have enough to do to believe firmly what baptism promises and brings—victory over death and the devil, forgiveness of sin, God's grace, the entire Christ, and the Holy Spirit with [the Spirit's] gifts."[24]

First of all, Luther dismisses the idea that baptism is simply some type of initiation and that after baptism something else is needed to keep in tune with God or to complete the baptism (confession or confirmation, for example).[25] In

Luther's day, works of penance were required in order to be found right with God. These works of penance (culminating in the indulgence controversy) had become more important than the sacrament of baptism itself. In the *Large Catechism*, Luther argues against such a belittling of baptism. He argues against Jerome:

> I say this to correct the opinion, which has long prevailed among us, that baptism is something past that we can no longer use after falling back into sin. This idea comes from looking only at the act that took place a single time. Indeed, St. Jerome is responsible for this view, for he wrote, "Penance is the second plank on which we must swim ashore after the ship founders," [the ship] in which we embarked when we entered the Christian community. This takes away the value of baptism, making it of no further use to us. Therefore it is incorrect to say this. The ship does not break up because, as we said, it is God's ordinance and not something that is ours. But it does happen that we slip and fall out of the ship. However, those who do fall out should immediately see to it that they swim to the ship and hold fast to it, until they can climb aboard again and sail on in it as before.[26]

Baptism is not just a one-time, past event that needs to be completed.[27] Of course, as an event, baptism happened at a particular moment in time and is a unique, singular event. It is not repeated, but the truth that it embodies demands an ongoing becoming, especially a becoming for us. In this sacrament, a journey begins, a spiritual baptism that lasts as long as life in this world lasts.

Baptism—or the work of the sacrament—is curiously not yet done. Those are Luther's words. As early as his treatise *The Babylonian Captivity of the Church*, Luther writes, "Vows should either be abolished by a general edict, especially those taken for life, and all [people] recalled to the vows of baptism, or else everyone should be diligently warned not to take a vow rashly. No one should be encouraged to do so; indeed, permission should be given only with difficulty and reluctance. For we have vowed enough in baptism, more than we can ever fulfill; if we give ourselves to the keeping of this one vow, we shall have all we can do."[28] Everything I do, everything I am, is dependent on the simple vows of baptism.[29]

> In this sacrament, a journey begins, a spiritual baptism that lasts as long as life in this world lasts.

When individuals remember their baptism, when they give thanks for the gift of forgiveness through the waters, they are not just looking back to some past event; they are not looking back at baptism as something that happened once and doesn't affect them now. On the contrary, they are remembering baptism as a present reality, as something that is continually calling them forward, inserting them not in self-constructed spiritualities but into God's plan, into God's life, into that hidden way. Baptism itself serves as a metaphor for God's action in life.

Through baptism, I enter into God's plan.[30] But God's plan is nothing other than death and resurrection. In this plan, God allies Godself to the baptized. That is, in a way, God adds Godself to their life. God opens up for them that hidden way that is God's plan flowing through the course of history, the Holy Spirit secretly weaving God's intent into everyday life. The opening up of God's way is not meant to bring about the fulfillment of my own dreams, give me a purpose-driven life, make me more successful, or whatever else I may value. This new beginning immerses me and the community of the baptized into discipleship. Baptism as an ongoing reality of their lives engages them continually in practice and exercise. The unique characteristic of this baptismal discipline or practice is not that it forms the baptized over time into a particular model of Christian, but that it incorporates them into God's plan of death and life, over which, of course, they have little control.

The baptized are inserted into the life of Jesus. To be inserted into the life of Jesus through baptism is really the same as drawing life from faith. I am inserted, placed in a marvelous field with beautiful boundaries, a garden, and this field engenders faith. At the heart of faith is Jesus Christ. Jesus and faith, I dare say, are actually the same. Through faith, I am in Jesus. Through faith, I know God. I taste the fullness, the wholeness, even in my incompleteness and searching.[31]

Faith itself, the presence of Jesus, is complete. Jesus gives himself to me completely, to each and every one completely, and in the community. I, though, continually try to set other parameters, create other gardens, and rely on other treasures, projects, and dreams. As I follow my own way, the Spirit continually returns in small signs and wonders, disrupting that way, disrupting myself, my plans and context, calling or sometimes even pushing me back. This is experienced as a type of death, as trauma. Experientia is living deep in that hidden way that the Holy Spirit traces. It is one of struggle and resistance, of confrontation and disruption, of dying and rising as the Holy Spirit awakens, nurtures, and increases faith in the heart.

In baptism, an individual is inserted into this hidden way, latent within history. According to Paul's use of dying and rising for baptism, the individual dies with Christ in order to be raised to new life with Christ. Though the traumatic realization of death (drowning) is real, one still finds themselves alive, having survived the death of God. The participation in the death of Christ ("fellowship of his pain," according to Cyril) is then also a participation in the survival of God's death on the cross, a death that is traumatically repeated throughout history until the end of time. It is as if death calls out—that is, not death itself, but that latent witness to God's death in the death of my neighbor, in the traumatic oppression of people, as, for example, in the enslavement of African Americans that continues to this day. Trauma grips an entire society. Every birth is a birth into the trauma of history.

Every human being is in solidarity, united in that trauma. Baptism names the traumatic foundation of human history. It does not let it rest or be ignored. Baptism reactualizes the trauma by rendering present the Christ event, but at the same time, in the naming, the individual is also immersed, inserted into God's hidden way in the midst of that trauma.

In baptism, at the communal and public beginning of this hidden way, as the Holy Spirit weaves my life through time and space, everything is rewritten or redefined: hopes and dreams, expectations and strivings. I no longer dream of worldly things, success, or fulfillment. Desire itself becomes something different. It is replaced by faith.

Luther writes about the desire to die: "In the first place you give yourself up to the sacrament of baptism and to what it signifies. That is, you desire to die, together with your sins, and to be made new at the Last Day. This is what the sacrament declares, as has been said. God accepts this desire at your hands and grants you baptism. From that hour [God] begins to make you a new person."[32]

This sentence can be terribly misinterpreted. The first inclination of human nature is to hear *sacrifice*. I must sacrifice myself in order to reach a particular goal. But this is not the intent of such a statement. Desire is perhaps best described outside usual reference points. It is the vigilance of faith. It is the abandonment of faith. It is the recognition of the trauma within history that no human being or system or theory or myth can contain, explain, or solve. It is the recognition of death already within life. It is a recognition of a call to die.

In that recognition, when I have tasted faith—the finest sweet wine—I do not want to go back to water or lite beer.[33] When I have discovered in the field the most precious treasure,

I sell everything else I own in order to buy that field. I die. That is, freely, spontaneously, without even realizing it, I enter the joy of God. I die to all that holds me captive and turned in on myself, including my most "holy" ideas about how I can become more spiritual or worthy. The proud die to their pride. The submissive die to their submissiveness. When God allows me to glimpse the hidden way, my life knows a disruption, a death that I gladly enter.

The desire to die is also the desire to be made new, but it doesn't happen without the dying. This is what the sacrament declares. Baptism is not just this beautiful event on a Sunday morning with white robes, pure water, candles, and well-dressed baptismal parties; it is an invitation into God's plan, this hidden, new way of dying and being made alive. Baptism defines not a spiritual practice or method that *I* have chosen but a way that I receive and welcome. In the hour of my baptism, as Luther puts it, God begins to make me a new person. God begins my own transfiguration through death. "This is my Son, the beloved; listen to him" (Luke 9:35). Or, as the baptismal liturgy proclaims to the newly baptized: "Child of God, you have been sealed by the Holy Spirit and marked with the cross of Christ forever."

When I have tasted faith— the finest sweet wine—I do not want to go back to water or lite beer.

In the *Small Catechism*, Luther writes, "What then is the significance of such a baptism with water? Answer: It signifies

122

that the old creature in us with all sins and evil desires is to be drowned and die through daily contrition and repentance, and on the other hand that daily a new person is to come forth and rise up to live before God in righteousness and purity forever."[34] Through baptism as a daily dying and new beginning, a new biography of my life is being written. The life of the baptized is dying and being pulled out daily. The events that assault me in life, the contradictions I endure, the people who interrupt (or cross) me, are all events in this daily dying, bringing me to a recognition of my ways, my self-sufficiency, my dependencies or stubbornness—contrition and repentance take place in my life in many forms. I can despair of all these events and contradictions. I can even ask "Why?" or "Why me?" but in a strange and wondrous way, I am continually immersed in the death of Jesus to be led on God's hidden way.

It is also here, in dying, that a new way is opened up, an unknown yet known way that is lived before God. This possibility, this new beginning, is constantly given, making every day new. Just as confession and repentance take on many forms, so is God's absolution, God's word of release, of freedom, of forgiveness given "in various ways and no one of them is to be despised for the sake of the others," Luther says.[35] Each life is lived in these continual new beginnings, always returning to baptism in order to make sense of life and death. I will not find meaning in the things the world cherishes—works, for example (even religious or spiritual works and practices)—no, but in baptism, in God's plan that is death to "my" meaning and resurrection to God's future.

Trauma and Prayer

This way begun in baptism, this dying and rising, faith, experientia, is what I have named spirituality—a baptismal spirituality. On this way, one's entire life is spiritual through the work, the action, the engagement, the irruption of the Holy Spirit. The immersion in water that constitutes baptism is now also an immersion in life's myriad disruptions: all those little deaths. Reflecting on baptism, Luther rewrites even the notion of death in another surprising passage:

> It follows, then, that baptism makes all sufferings, and especially death, profitable and helpful, so that they simply . . . serve baptism in the doing of its work, that is, in the slaying of sin. It cannot be otherwise. For [the one] who would fulfill the work and purpose of baptism and be rid of sin, must die. Sin, however, does not like to die, and for this reason it makes death so bitter and so horrible.[36]

Such a statement requires some contextualization. In a world where spirits, good or bad, permeated all of life and encountered the living through the various events of their lives, it was easy to say that suffering or death was caused by a force beyond one's control.[37] Theodicy was not yet a question in the sixteenth century. God caused suffering or death either for the betterment or for the punishment of humankind. "God" was like a gap-filler. Wherever something could not be explained reasonably or rationally, God became the reason.

This enchanted world of course has been left behind, though many today still use God to explain or rationalize events and ideologies. Yet, suffering and death are not weapons or instruments God uses to accomplish God's plan. So, how is one to approach suffering and death? When God is not the ultimate go-to solution for everything, how is God's presence in this world rethought? How is Luther's comment that baptism makes suffering and even death profitable and helpful to be understood?

At this point, it is good to recall how the spiritual life is framed, its context. Faith is poured out into one's heart at baptism, and the journey on a hidden way begins, both known and unknown. Faith gives Jesus. Faith doesn't cling to a God up in the heavenly heights but reaches out to a God hidden on the cross. Faith reaches out to what the heart, the mind, the soul cannot capture or contain, no matter how rational or sophisticated the philosophical or theological system might be. The reality of suffering illustrates this well. To a certain degree, theologians have domesticated suffering. They have incorporated suffering into a system. Some may have subscribed to a theodicy that "explains" suffering. This is what I mean by domestication: taking something that is actually inaccessible, incomprehensible, and fitting it into a system that gives the illusion of representing, understanding, and thereby mastering it. Yet, suffering cannot be explained or represented.[38] Suffering is that which disrupts all attempts at systematization. The cross stands as a sign: as suffering, as death, it silences all explanations. Selah.

Yet, I will try my best at an explanation. All my attempts, however, merely turn God into something calculable, something I can manipulate to avoid the threat and danger of God. I believe human attempts at explanation simply want to avoid suffering as it encounters the community in the neighbor and in the world.

> The cross stands as a sign: as suffering, as death, it silences all explanations.

Suffering is the one construct I cannot quite fit in anywhere, so I (and the community) will explain it away. The blame is placed on constructions, such as disobedience to God's law, or it is argued that suffering is actually necessary for salvation, for grace, for gospel.

When Luther writes that suffering and death are profitable, isn't he too leaning toward such easy explanations? No, I believe not. Luther is not attempting to explain suffering or death, nor is he giving them a purpose; instead, he is writing about a radically different relationship that is established with them through baptism. Long before Bonhoeffer wrote that God is not a God of the gaps, Luther points to the same insight, and he does so through the sacraments. For in the sacrament the incarnate God is encountered, the God who comes not just as a word that is heard but as a body that is touched, tasted, smelled, and seen. God comes not as someone distinct from suffering and death but as one who is encountered in it. The significance of the sacrament, the meaning of baptism, implies a radical shift in the relationship to life; it rewrites the relationship I have to both fullness and emptiness, to completeness and incompleteness, including my relationship to suffering and death.

God does not serve as an answer to all questions, filling in all of the gaps of knowledge or reason. God is the one who changes the way I am situated in the world, the space I occupy, even the questions I ask. God changes the very meaning of desire and need. "Even the darkness is not dark to you; the night is as bright as the day, for darkness is as light to you" (Ps 139:12).

In baptism, a journey of faith begins, a journey that the Spirit is continually tracing for the faithful. On that journey, suffering and death are encountered, sometimes continually. Suffering and death are encountered daily in the many small disruptions of life. But they also are encountered in bigger upheavals such as natural disasters, a pandemic, terminal illness, torture, violence, rape, and murder. They are experienced in many forms by all people. These upheavals, big and small, are not caused by God. They confront all people with the traumatic, with that which cannot be captured or controlled in life, to that which is strangely latent in all things. I cannot dismiss them, explain them away, or avoid them; instead, the community and I are called to step into them. As someone living more or less in faith, the only response I can have toward suffering and death is a ministry of bearing them, carrying them, being in solidarity with suffering and death, a fellowship in the pain.

Baptism has opened a way in which suffering and death are looked squarely in the face, acknowledged, confronted, and rectified (where possible), but never avoided or explained away. Baptism is not baptism in the River Jordan but baptism into the suffering, into the death, of Jesus; into the suffering, into the death, of the neighbor. In baptism, as the community (communion, fellowship) walks on this new, hidden way, it enters into suffering and death, not just its own (which only risks being self-centered) but that of its neighbor. In stepping into suffering and death, in the midst of daily dying, each and every one hears again the voice at baptism: "You are my child, my beloved." For the baptized, suffering and death never have the last word.

Luther continues in his reflection to draw a contrast between this communion, or participation, in suffering and the ease and prosperity of the life culture has made into an goal, an idol, a god: "Because for all who are baptized, their baptism has made the repose, ease, and prosperity of this life a very poison and a hindrance to its work. For in the easy life no one learns to suffer, to die with gladness, to get rid of sin, and to live in harmony with baptism. Instead there grows only love of this life and horror of eternal life, fear of death and unwillingness to blot out sin."[39]

What is to be feared is a glorified life that avoids or denies suffering. What is to be feared is the god of such a life: a romantic, all-white, and sparkling Jesus. What is to be feared is a glorified spirituality that is nothing other than self-seeking, a self-fulfillment, a nurturing of one's own spirit, an illusory letting go of the ego that only strengthens the ego even more.

Baptism has opened a way of life contrary to the ways of the world. It has opened the way to a communion into the death and into the life of Jesus, into the trauma of history, and into God's hidden way. The life begun in baptism—new creation—is a communion into the open wound of Jesus and the neighbor. There, in the wound of Jesus, the community hears God's voice. There, in the wound of the other, of the neighbor, I hear Jesus calling. Baptism is immersion into the suffering and into the life of God, and so also immersion into the suffering of the world. When a person is baptized and made into a child of God, when they are baptized and made into a new person, when they are baptized and become part of the communion of saints, that communion is defined by the suffering of the neighbor. The suffering of the world becomes their suffering. The communion is universal.

> The life begun in baptism—new creation—is a communion into the open wound of Jesus and the neighbor.

Baptism is this radical reorientation of life. Communion in the suffering of the neighbor, in the wounded world, is living fully the human condition. It is the vigilance of living in all the joys and yet all the limitations of the created world. Living fully the human condition is living obediently in the space and time God has given. It means living in a communion of saints, a communion of neighbors, of bodies, of suffering, of death. It means practicing dying. The community is not a gathering of privileged individuals who have been "saved" (or pulled out of the world) but those who are thrust back in, who belong wholly, totally, to the world.[40]

The beautiful liturgical procession with lighted vigil candles walks not triumphantly to the high altar but quietly, in fear and faith, out in the street. Baptism has redefined desire and life. Baptism sets the community on a road where it is continually confronted by many little deaths, but also sustained by the resurrection, by the promise of God, in the midst of these deaths. "Therefore this whole life is nothing else than a spiritual baptism which does not cease," writes Luther, until the day I physically die.

5

Communal Prayer

God in the Midst

In this reflection on spirituality through the lens of baptism, prayer, and the Psalms, a particular religious cosmology has been developed. God is not a figure "up in heaven," but down here in the messiness, the chaos, the disorder, and the suffering, as well as in the joys, the laughter, and the contentment of life. God is not a fill-in-the gap god, but one who sometimes quietly and sometimes not-so-quietly permeates all of life. God is not an object—like a cross hung on a sanctuary wall to be worshipped—but the one continually in the midst of the world, reconciling, reclaiming, and renewing it. God's presence may be so hidden that one can conclude God is absent. But God's absence is precisely God's call, the one who accompanies the despondent disciples, who breaks bread with them, who touches them in ways no one else can, and sets them off on their way.

Though the heart may be empty or full, God pours faith into the heart from which a person draws life.

The faith poured out is a communion in the righteousness of God (to use more theological language) or into the love, the reconciliation, that God engenders in life. In faith, I am one with God. Faith fulfills the first commandment—you shall have no other gods—for faith makes God all in all. I am placed in a marvelous field, a beautiful garden, defined by God's command.

Yet, in this life, on this new way, I am enticed by other gods to make detours. Paul's imagery, particularly in Romans and 1 Corinthians, is starker. Struggle in this life, to Paul, is a cosmic battle in which Satan—or the evil one, or the evil forces or powers and principalities—fight against God's plan of new birth, reconciliation, and renewal. In 1 Corinthians 2:8, Paul writes, "The rulers of this age . . . crucified the Lord of glory." On the cross, God confronts Satan and his hosts.[1] God meets all the forces of oppression and dehumanization. The cross is the battlefield and also the place of God's ultimate victory. Again, in 1 Corinthians 15:25, Paul looks forward to that day when Christ will rule and place all his enemies under his feet.

Human beings find themselves in the midst of this cosmic battle. They are the playing field for the struggle between Satan and Christ, between the powers and principalities and God's new creation. This struggle is experienced in my body, not only in my spirit.

Too often I let the garden go to waste (to return to the imagery of Ps 16 and the boundaries God has marked for each person). The boundaries of my garden become blurred or the markers become hidden. I seek other goals and self-imagined fulfillment. Sometimes I do so consciously; many times I do so unconsciously, driven by emotions or unknown trauma or by my body or by the many myths I carry from culture, religion, or race. Whether I seek fulfillment in culturally accepted values (family, money, prestige, power) or through addiction, God is pushed to the side or relegated, boxed in, and locked up to just one part of *my* identity.

I resist the movement, the obedience, into which faith invites me. I want to do it my way. When, however, the Spirit enters in, the Spirit bends what is inflexible, fires what is cold and languishing, calls back what has gone astray,[2] and then my desire becomes faith; I die gladly to all that is stubborn within me, and I taste the sweetness of the Spirit's hidden way. This is experientia. It becomes teacher and guide, better than any study or book.

Experientia is the continual molding of life by the Holy Spirit. I am not always cognitively aware of this molding; perhaps I only sense or intuit or taste that blessedness secretly stirring my heart. This blessedness, Luther notes, is known only in faith and experientia.[3] Other words can describe this blessedness. It is the joy experienced when the treasure is found in the field, when the finest and most precious pearl is discovered among many fake gems. It is the sweetness of God's law, finer than the sweetest wine. It is tears of thanksgiving when returning from the streets, from a confrontation with armed soldiers, from exile to safety. It is the joy of communion as a community bears one another along the way. All of these and more are experiences of the hidden, secret way that the Holy Spirit weaves throughout history.

In this life, it is difficult to find words for the immeasurable goodness, the serene joy that is faith poured out into the heart. I am speechless before God (*unaussprechlich*, or literally "not-speak-able," as Luther puts it). What can I say? What can the community sing? My heart, my life, wishes to express its profoundest cry, its deepest lament, its most exuberant shouts of joy before God, but what expression can I or the community give to those dimensions of the heart that will intensify the silence and not violate it or attempt to control it? How do I move through and with all dimensions of human emotion toward the truth of a communion, reconciliation, into that deep-seated thanksgiving? What shape and form does the Holy Spirit inhabit? What utterance intervenes into a speechless context?

The community doesn't have to look far to find a language that would express the multiple dimensions of experientia. It already has been immersed in that language; the Psalms give it a language. In the preface to his Psalms commentary, Luther writes that in the Psalms the community has a better example than all the examples of the saints, because the Psalter doesn't just give stories about the saints (what they did, etc.) but reveals their life and struggles: "These holy ones spoke with God with great seriousness in the most critical situations. The Psalter doesn't just give us their words over their works but shows also their heart and the innermost treasure of their soul, so that we can see into the foundation and source of their words and works, that is, into their heart. There we see what thoughts they had, how their heart faced and held up in the midst of danger and distress."[4]

The Psalms reveal how the holy ones speak with God. But for Luther, *reden* (to speak) connotes much more than just speaking. This speaking is from the heart; it reveals the heart and involves the whole person in their relationship to God. Of course, Luther writes, he prefers hearing the words of holy persons more than just seeing their works, but "it is even more dear to me to see the heart and the treasure of their soul than to hear their words."[5]

The Psalter gives an insight into the heart and treasure of the faith-filled soul. For the community that identifies as Christian, the Psalter

> The Psalms reveal how the holy ones speak with God.

also gives the heart and treasure of Jesus's soul. In giving God's word, the Psalter, through the Holy Spirit, molds that faith community into the word, into that heart and treasure. "Then the Psalter is nothing else than a school and exercise of affect."[6] Human affections are shaped by the affections it reveals. The Psalter gives a language, words that are far more than words: it gives silent words that resonate throughout the earth, revealing a secret, hidden way, a life that touches the foundation and source—a life of faith. The Psalter gives all this to the community that meditates on it, sings and speaks and dances, recites and studies it.

In the prayers for peace that the young people in East Germany organized throughout the 1980s, Psalm 85 played a central role. It often was sung. It appeared again and again in many of the prayers, like a mantra or as an anchor.

Psalm 85 describes the promise with words that were important to those living in East Germany, in a society of distrust, injustice, and fear. Righteousness, peace, mercy, and truth were sweet words with which they grappled in discussions, in meditations, in sermons, in prayers, and in song. They asked haunting questions: What is righteousness? "Is it standing alongside those who hide in the shadow of power and prosperity or is it standing by the side of the powerless, the suffering ones? Or are these just two sides of ourselves?" They brought righteousness into dialogue with freedom, which for them was a necessary attribute of peace. They asked: "What does a society look like that links righteousness and freedom?"[7] Or in the words of Psalm 85, what does a society look like in which righteousness and peace kiss?

Psalm 85 pulled them into a language of faith and into a deep hope in the promise that they knew did not depend on them, their worthiness, or their ability to pray or take action. Psalm 85 pulled them into God's truth—that is, God's faithfulness to the promise of mercy, of reconciliation, of peace. In this promise, they were strengthened. God's truth, Jesus Christ, is mercy.

The Psalms pull the community into prayer. They do so with some distinct patterns. Psalm 85, for example, begins in thanksgiving, moves to beseeching and pleading, and then to prophecy, the fulfillment of the promise. In his commentary on this psalm, Luther admonishes the reader to learn the pattern well. "You too learn the way to pray and teach. Before praying give thanks, and before teaching pray. Then you will go about it in the right way, as this psalm did."[8] Here teaching is also called prophecy: foretelling and proclaiming the promise.

These actions—thanksgiving, praying, prophecy (eschatological hope)—can be engaged on one's own, but they take on a new dimension when they are practiced communally. Faith is communal. Through baptism I become part of a communion of saints that participates in the suffering of the world—that bears, that carries, that steps into that suffering. God's truth and

> The Psalms pull the community into prayer.

mercy are inherently communal. The community of the faithful always has gathered, if even behind locked doors, to give thanks, to remember, to pray, and to hope. The faith community is marked by that hope.

The second commandment calls to this thanksgiving and prayer: you are not to misuse the name of your God. "What is this?" Luther asks. Answer: "We are to fear and love God, so that we do not curse, swear, practice magic, lie, or deceive using God's name, but instead use that very name in every time of need to call on, pray to, praise, and give thanks to God." This is mirrored in the first petition of the Lord's Prayer: may your name be hallowed. In the *Small Catechism*, Luther comments, "It is true that God's name is holy in itself, but we ask in this prayer that it may also become holy in and among us."[9] Making God's name holy in and among the community happens as the Holy Spirit conforms the community, molds it, shapes it into Jesus Christ.

This formation happens as faith draws people together to form a community of thanksgiving and prayer.

Vigilance

Throughout this exploration of spirituality and prayer, I have focused on what God is doing, how the Holy Spirit is molding you, me, and the community through events, situations, and persons in life. Luther has called this molding experientia. I have also called it a baptismal spirituality or baptismal discipline. All of life is a spiritual baptism. As mentioned, the work of the Holy Spirit takes on a communal form. In the depth of prayer, I discover that I am not alone; there is always another: Jesus Christ. A fellowship is created in baptism. The fellowship becomes visible. It became visible in the small prayer groups in East Germany, when two or three, or four or five, got together to express something before God.

Communal prayer is a place of this shaping by the Holy Spirit. But what does such a communal prayer look like? How have Christians gathered to pray, and what did they do then? I have pointed to one example from East Germany, but there are many others throughout history—and such a variety. To take a glimpse at the early church, as Christians gathered for prayer under another form of brutal oppression and persecution, a very simple but deeply theological pattern developed.

There is little doubt that the early church was concerned with the regularity of prayer, though there was also a great deal of variety in the way the early church understood that rhythm or regularity.[10] In these nascent communities, an intense concern is witnessed: How does the Christ event, the paschal mystery, become a reality in daily life? This question encompassed all of life in this world. The life, death, and resurrection of Jesus Christ is not reduced to simply assuring the salvation of the individual soul. The Christ event is the salvific moment, the crux, of all creation. The metanoia, the reversal, the disruption that the Holy Spirit effects in the lives of individuals is also a metanoia for all of creation. In fact, the life and prayer of the baptized brings to expression the cry of all creation.[11] When the community gathers for prayer, that prayer envelopes and addresses a community much larger than just the individuals who participate.

> The Christ event is the salvific moment, the crux, of all creation.

Faithfully engaging in a particular rhythm of prayer expressed a deep waiting of the community, waiting along with all of creation. Prayer was not just a spiritual discipline that individuals practiced in order to be more attuned to God in their life or to fill up the gas tank. It was not considered a work or a good deed by which a person might be saved or sanctified. As Paul Bradshaw writes, "the observance of fixed times of daily prayer in the early Christian community was none other than the liturgical expression of constant readiness for, and expectation of, the Parousia."[12] And even when the expected Parousia did not materialize as first anticipated, the community's expectant waiting was sublimated into a new understanding of time: every event, if you will, no matter how ordinary, may be God's Parousia.

This expectancy had profound implications for the community. Because every event could bear the coming of the Lord, Christians did not withdraw from the world but became more embodied in it. *Embodied* is Bradshaw's term: "The realization that the new age had already begun was embodied in the eucharistia for what God had done, constant readiness for the Kingdom of God was embodied in regular petition for its final consummation, and participation in the apostolic mission to the world was embodied in intercession for the salvation of all [humankind]."[13]

Daily prayer is embodiment of a vigilance and patience, a silence and solidarity that faith engenders within the heart—within one's whole being, mind, emotions, body. Daily prayer and communal prayer render a community differently to what is around it. Its spaces are opened wide, incorporating the whole cosmos into the life of the praying community. Its expectations of space and time are turned inside out. Rather than seen as limits set on creativity, rather than realities that a community might fear, a community's situation in time has a new vocation: space and time, the environment, earth and waters, sky and cosmos, are the arena of God's coming.

Time is one of God's more peculiar creative activities. Its peculiarity is that through time, God offers human beings the possibility of ever-new beginnings. Today, everything is different! Claude Tresmontant writes that time is nothing but a concept signifying that God has not given everything at once, but that God's creative activity is unceasing, always inventing, little by little.[14] God's continual creative activity—new creation—is ever-new beginnings, in continual metanoia, giving life, forgiving sins, reconciling. God reclaims all creation, but not all at once. God traces a hidden way throughout history. The Holy Spirit sanctifies, makes holy. Baptism signifies this continual creative activity, and its ongoing reality is what Luther has called a spiritual baptism.

Communal prayer, through vigilance and patience, embodies time as an arena of God's creative activity. It is the expectation of Christ's return, and through such a prayer the faith community becomes more attuned to the unexpected in everyday living. Prayer, and in particular the Psalms, trains the community to be attentive to both the temporal and eternal, the visible and invisible irruptions of the Holy Spirit. That which often is dismissed as unimportant, momentary, fleeting, insignificant, marginal, or just plain uninteresting suddenly can be truly significant: an event, a person, a situation that bears the anticipated one. My relation to the world and the neighbor is broadened, heightened, widened, deepened. It is turned inside out. Now the center of God's action is not just in me but in the community, in the neighbor, in the world.

> God offers human beings the possibility of ever-new beginnings. Today, everything is different!

As communal prayer developed throughout late antiquity, particularly in the East, the morning hour of prayer took on a penitential tone expressed in the bodily gesture of kneeling and in the increasing use of Psalm 51 as a morning psalm.[15] For the praying community, the day begins in the recognition of one's place in creation. The day begins in the continual hope and assurance of God's mercy. It is as if the day begins in an attentiveness to relationship, to the network of persons, institutions, environments, and the social web that surrounds each person and calls on a deep attitude of humility.

Through the practice of daily prayer, the community is invited into a new orientation in time and space. Time and space are not simply *a priori* conditions or a frame within which life happens. Time and space are experienced as invitations by God into God's continual creative activity. Time and space become witnesses to the gospel. The liturgy encourages the community of faith to exercise these reversals, to enter ever more deeply into this gospel rhythm. This reorientation of ordinary timekeeping does not remove the believer or the community from the world. On the contrary, the community is better able to engage the world and its struggle because it is not oppressed or captive to the world. The community is placed more directly in the midst of the world's agony and beauty. Communal prayer practices place the community in a metanoia, a continual reversal and reorientation. Communal prayer does not isolate but throws the community back into the world.

> Communal prayer does not isolate but throws the community back into the world.

Luther's definition of prayer (Chapter 3) as an activity that drives away all evil is not only true for an individual life but for all creation. Communal prayer, in other words, rehearses the victory won by Christ, the victory of life over death, the victory of mercy over sin, the victory of reconciliation over separation. It is the victory of a communion that is God's faithfulness throughout history to all people and all creation.

A Simple Pattern

At this point, I want to shift more explicitly to the form of communal prayer. The pattern of prayer will clarify even further the spiritual characteristic of prayer. When I speak about pattern or form, however, I need to make a disclaimer. The form of communal prayer is not uniform. Liturgical historians have, over and over, insisted on this truth. There is not one form of prayer or worship in the early church that can simply be imitated.

A technique or regularized practice always will embody a metaphysic,[16] or a theology. In so doing, it can also bend, contort, or sometimes suspend the metaphysic and propose something new. The technique actually disrupts the metaphysical to focus one's gaze on the incarnational. I want to expand the argument and say that every form or pattern also directs those who engage in it to their bodies, to the physical (not just metaphysical). In the physical, I encounter the theological embodied. I discover truth as mercy, as communion. A pattern of prayer, therefore, is not inherently a rule or law imposed (though this is how it often is experienced) but rather an embodied theology. A form or pattern also can proclaim or preach.

One characteristic of communal prayer, noted by several major liturgical historians, was the great simplicity of its form or structure.[17] Communal prayer basically consisted of two things: psalms and prayers. This was particularly true of the monastic office, but also of the so-called cathedral office in the city church.

For those who might not be familiar with this classification, the daily office has been classically divided into three types: the monastic office, with its origin primarily in Egyptian monasticism; the cathedral office, which was primarily morning and evening prayer in the city, celebrated usually at the cathedral (the city's main church) and for all the baptized; and the urban monastic office (when the monks came in from the desert to the city), which was a hybrid office modifying some of the strict monastic practice and adapting it with elements from the cathedral office. It is not possible to identify one pattern that fits all three of these models. Scholars have amply shown how many variations exist from place to place, from city to city, and from region to region. Rightly so, especially if daily prayer is to be the prayer of a people in their context. The monastic office, particularly rooted in the Egyptian tradition, is characterized by prayers (offices) held throughout the day and night. The Psalms were recited in a continuous fashion, from the beginning to the end of the Psalter, without regard for time of day or season of the liturgical year. At the other extreme was the cathedral office, with only two times of prayer: matins and vespers, morning and evening prayer, which consisted in certain fixed psalms reflecting the time of day and other psalms according to the time of year (sometimes chosen in a continuous manner). The cathedral office also included certain ritual actions, such as the lighting of the lamps for evening prayer (vespers).

What is most significant, when contrasted with some contemporary practices of communal prayer, is the simple structure of the daily office: psalms and prayers. There is not always strong evidence for a Scripture reading. In the cathedral office there would be a hymn or two, but the fundamental pattern of communal prayer was primarily anchored in psalmody and prayer. For many Protestants, and particularly for my own denomination (Lutheran), the apparent absence of Scripture reading from the pattern of communal prayer seems shocking. Yet, the word isn't absent. For the Psalms themselves are God's word given to the community. In the Psalms, God addresses the community; the community is taught this unique language, which also becomes its prayer. The word molds and shapes the community with prayer through the Psalms.

In fact, the alternation of psalmody and prayer is particularly significant in the monastic office. In the earliest texts concerning the shape of the monastic office, mostly found in the writings of John Cassian (c. 360–c. 435) and his description of the Egyptian office,[18] psalmody and prayer were intricately woven together in almost a call and response form. In almost a call and response form, a tapestry of psalms, of intense and prolonged silences and fervent prayer. For example, one of the sources of Benedict's Rule, the Rule of the Master, clearly indicates this alternation between psalmody and prayer. Every psalm culminated in a time of silence that even occasionally included prostration on the part of at least the one reciting the psalm. Father Adalbert de Vogüé comments that unfortunately there remains almost nothing of this prayer in current practice, whether monastic or cathedral.

The time of prayer following every psalm was to be unique, a moment of great intensity when the language of the psalm would resonate deep within those praying. In certain practices, it appears as if the psalm was sung not communally but by one person with everyone else attentively listening. The ensuing prayer demanded an "intense effort of supplication," as de Vogüé puts it.[19] All the energy of both body and soul were mobilized in this act of prayer. As the Rule of St. Benedict was quoted, tears would flow and hands would stretch out as if clinging to the feet of Christ. The silence and prayer concluding the psalm was far more than just a prescribed prayer; it intensified the psalm itself. The psalm's language and metaphors now irrupt in the midst of the assembly. In fact, there are indications that this silence and prayer were engaged spontaneously by anyone who was deeply moved as they listened to the psalm. If the gathering of monks was sitting, that person would stand up to pray. If the assembly was already standing, that person would prostrate themselves on the floor. It is clear for de Vogüé that it was this prayer itself, following the psalm, that constituted the chief part of the daily office.[20] In the silence and prayer, the psalm became the language of the community through one of its members.

De Vogüé finds the structure of communal prayer so radical that he believes it destabilizes the modern distinction between private prayer and liturgical prayer, between the private recitation of the Psalms and the communal recitation. For the monks, the liturgy of the hours was precisely a place where the continuous prayer of the day, the personal recitation of the Psalms and Scripture during the workday, was seamlessly integrated into the time of communal prayer. The communal prayer is only unique in that it is verbalized, audible. The prayer that concludes each psalm in the daily office is not a simple liturgical incantation but a prayer of the heart. The prayer said outside the common (liturgical) office, the prayer said during work and throughout the course of everyday living—that prayer is not an appetizer for liturgical prayer but, according to de Vogüé, the heart itself of communal prayer. Meditating on God's law day and night in the silence of one's heart and singing that law in the midst of the assembly is one continuous activity.

But I would expand de Vogüé's insight even further: the prayer of individuals shaped the community. In the communal prayer of the monks, the recitation of a psalm and prayerful intercession often were accomplished by an individual rather than by an assembly singing or praying together. The role of this individual in communal prayer, as the one responsible in a given moment for the prayer of the entire assembly, suggests a unique way in which community itself was deeply affected and formed through the prayer (the spiritual life) of each participant.

One of the greatest complaints often levied at so-called liturgical worship is its impersonality. The individual is simply a participant-observer, following the lead of a presider or two. Though attempts are made that the liturgy be a time of active participation, the regular Sunday or weekday participant is often merely an observer. Of course, Sunday worship in a faith community cannot be compared to the dynamics of a monastic community. But, in the witness of this early form of monastic praying, as each individual is called on and engaged in the communal act, all faith communities are challenged to reflect on how each participant is responsible for the liturgical progression of prayer. The liturgy is submitted or handed over to the assembly. The voice of one participant, which for me is always the voice of the other, addresses the assembly through the psalm. That person becomes a free voice, and the whole assembly is continuously addressed by the other's voice, by the neighbor—now not in a text but through a living voice in the community's midst. Through the recitation of the psalm, each participant is given a language for prayer, and this prayer becomes the cry, the lament or the praise, the anguish or the joy, in which a community is constituted.

> The liturgy is submitted or handed over to the assembly.

The Psalms as language, as an external word, provide a structure for praying at every moment, and in this way they bridge a gap between the personal and the communal, the private and the liturgical. The liturgy itself is opened and becomes extremely vulnerable to this spontaneous interaction, prayer, irruption, and utterance of the Holy Spirit.

Psalmody and Prayer

What is the relationship between psalmody and prayer? Bonhoeffer states that the Psalms are both God's word to human beings and subsequently also the words of their prayer to God.[21] This insight is important. The idea that prayer is simply a movement initiated by a pray-er toward God is debunked: the very words of prayer are first given by God. The Spirit is the one who prays within each person. Bonhoeffer, rooted in Luther's thought, recalls that prayer is taught in the school of the Psalter.

For the early monastic community, the Psalms were God's word addressed to them. The role of the psalm as God's word explains in part the absence of any formal reading of Scripture in the office (though there are other reasons for this absence in the monastic structure, especially the admonition to a *lectio continua*). God's word in the Psalms is not simply read; it is sung and engaged with by those gathered. The use of the psalm also takes on a preparatory function within the daily office. That is, the psalm as God's word trains the community in its essential task: prayer. This preparation is on one level an introductory instruction; it is teaching the community what prayer is, how to pray, and what language to use. The language of the Psalms becomes the language of the community through the prayer, through silence—selah!—through gesture, music, praise, and supplication.

But the Psalms also have a disruptive function. As in the practice of the early monastic communities, the Psalms embody a voice addressed to the entire assembly, a voice that comes from outside, a voice, an utterance, over which the assembly has no control. Through this transmission, the Psalms broaden the horizon of the community through time and place while, in the same instance, directing the community to a voice that is not in their midst. The Psalms, as external word, register a continual return, an utterance of the Spirit, an irruption in the assembly's midst.

The utterance and irruption affects the body as individuals and as a community. An intriguing text in a sermon by Césaire d'Arles (470–542, archbishop of Arles and saint) states, "Singing the psalms is like sowing in a field; praying (*orare*) is like digging deeply into the field where we recover the seed a second time through this labor (*arando*)."[22] *Orare*, or praying, is of course also speaking, pleading, begging, and it is described as a labor, *arando*—literally plowing and cultivating the field. Prayer is a profound assimilation of the Psalms into one's life. Through this plowing, the word spoken or sung in the psalm is acquired. Through prayer, the Psalms become the voice of the community. The community acquires them—that is, the word expressed in the Psalms shapes, transforms, transfigures, and reorients the community toward God and toward the other.

But there is another connotation to this little word *arando*. *Arando* also can be the furrowing of an old face or of aged skin, the wrinkling of the body. If I improvise the meaning of the word, another dimension of prayer is discovered. Prayer is not simply an intellectual activity, nor is it a verbal activity that might touch the heart. It is not simply an emotional activity that strikes me in one moment with a particular movement of the soul and then passes on, like a beautiful sunset that I cannot recapture. The Psalms through prayer dig deep furrows on my skin; they plow my body. They mark my body, and I carry that mark everywhere. Prayer is God's work of plowing the field of the heart, opening it up to faith.

The voice addressed to the community in the Psalms calls on all the resources of body and soul. Both body and soul are marked by that word. This approach to prayer as plowing and as marking, like a

> Prayer is God's work of plowing the field of the heart, opening it up to faith.

tattoo or even a wound on the body, echoes centuries later in Luther's own approach to prayer as that place where the word is exercised. Meditation is thinking about the word, planting the word, disputing with the word, and Luther cites Psalm 37:30, "*Os iusti meditabitur sapientiam*" (The mouth of the just will speak wisdom).[23] The Psalms through meditation become my speech. Luther also uses an analogy from Augustine for this action, this labor (*arando*). Just as chirping (*garrire*) is the occupation of the birds, so is this meditation the true work of the human being: a profound engagement with the word and with words. Luther, that great commentator and reader and singer of the Psalms, understood, as any dedicated monk would, this ancient practice of the voice carried by the psalm irrupting into the context of the community, shaping the individual and the community.

Curiously, Luther translates *meditari* with the German *reden*, or "speaking." This curiosity provides a critical insight into how Luther understands both meditation and speaking, and speaking is not just any action for Luther. Speech, the ability to speak and to meditate, distinguishes human beings from all other creatures.[24] But isn't meditation more than just speaking? Isn't it also silence? Watching? Vigilance? Does Luther reduce meditation to simply spoken words?

Speaking/meditation for Luther implies a confrontation with words, with the text, with Scripture, with the word encountered in everyday life (see Chapter 3). Speaking/meditation is arguing with the words, being disputed by them, as well as simply talking. Speaking is *nachdenken*: reflecting, pondering, mulling over. It is an activity of the heart that is first provoked by a word spoken to it.

When God speaks, when God reveals God's self in the word, in Jesus Christ, the playing field (the vocation) of human beings is defined as an exercise of the word.[25] This is not simply a rational activity[26] but one that engages the whole human being—the heart (intellect, emotions, body)—in a struggle: speaking with and against God, resisting and submitting to the Holy Spirit.

This speaking through the Scripture reveals the heart to the pray-er, the heart shaped by faith. Speech and meditation are both this deeply private, individual activity whereby I am shaped by the word and by a very public manifestation or witness, because every heart—the manner in which I am in the world—flows directly from this shaping. The witness given in this world is one rooted in my own struggle, meditation, and disputation with the word. Through this struggle, the treasure of faith is revealed to those around me and to the community.

The Psalms embody this meditation, speech, and struggle. And proclamation in fact stems from meditation that reveals the treasure of the heart God has shaped.

A New Language

What happens in the alternation between psalmody and prayer? The dynamic of the Holy Spirit is revealed. In the psalmody—in singing, reading, and meditating on the Psalms—the community is immersed into God's own word. It is taught a language of prayer, but also a language of life, a communal language.

In the Psalms, God's voice, God's utterance, intervenes in my contexts, in my heart, in my self. This intervention, this voice of God thundering, breaks open my self-constructed worlds with its values. This intervention is not without struggle, as I have shown. It is the beginning of meditation. Curiously, the voice that intervenes becomes my own voice, my own words. God encompasses me in such a way that God works always as an intervention in the deepest fibers of my being. Bonhoeffer writes that God's word, God's voice in Jesus, becomes a voice that addresses us and that uniquely becomes our own voice.[27]

Many people who have tried praying the Psalms complain because they can't identify with the text. That is precisely the point. The text is not meant to fit my identity or accommodate me in my contexts. In the Psalms I am addressed by a voice that kills and makes alive; that reshapes, remolds, and reorients my identity; that makes of me a new creation. The Psalms reveal a voice that irrupts, that encounters me, that disrupts: the voice of the neighbor who calls out to me, the voice of the other who awakens me. I cannot control that voice. The Spirit blows where it wills. And here, in the Psalms, the whole community and I are already being trained to listen to it.

Bonhoeffer writes that the first concern I should have when approaching the Psalms—before I ask what they mean for me—is to ask what they have to do with Jesus Christ.[28] The intervention of word in the psalm is like an awakening. The voice awakens me out of a dream and shapes me in a new language. The dream I create for myself, of course, is a dream that avoids death, confrontation, and disruption. In the context the community (and I) creates for itself, suffering is eliminated. My natural self does not want to die. Sin in me resists death. Whoever heard of sin that wants to die? The Psalms, however, confront and exercise me with death and with the death of my neighbor. Is this the reason that the communion of saints through the ages has made the Psalms central to Christian prayer?

In the Psalms, God gives a new language for prayer and for life. God gives, first of all, a language for prayer. God gives the words for prayer. God teaches us how to pray in the Psalms. Here God lays before the community of pray-ers all the needs, concerns, cares, burdens, and the joys of this world. God names all these for the community in prayer, a prayer that becomes the community's own.

But God gives more. God gives in the Psalms not only a language for prayer but a language through which I get to know who I am. The words of the Psalms, spoken from the outside to me, enable me to discover the depth of my self, the image in which God has created and redeemed me.

As a young man, I once had the opportunity to complete the thirty-day Ignatian retreat (thirty days of silence). Alone, in conversation with my spiritual adviser, the word in the Scripture and the Psalms began giving me a new context in which my life took shape. This word from Psalm 16 has shaped a large part of my own reflection on faith, baptism, and prayer. In Psalm 16:6, I read (from the Gelineau Psalter): "The boundary lines have fallen for me in pleasant places; I have a goodly heritage." When I walked outside, I observed the winter forest: the trees silent and bare of leaves, the sky gray and foggy. And I thought, *What a marvelous creation!* Despite the absence of all things I might consider pleasing or beautiful (luscious verdure, singing birds, forest flowers, blue skies, and warm, sunny air), despite the apparent dreariness of the landscape, this winter forest had everything it needed simply to be, and it was beautiful. What, then, about my life? Isn't it the same? Despite the failings, despite the things that I don't like about myself, despite all my own struggles, what God has given me—the field, the heritage, the playing space, the context, the vocation God has provided—is enough! It is beautiful. I will find everything I need right there. The boundary lines have indeed fallen for me in pleasant places.

The language God gives in the Psalms awakens me to this reality of a life lived in God. This language reveals a landscape far broader than any I ever could have imagined. The Psalms reveal the treasure, the source of all words and works, all emotions and thoughts, all physical strivings and hindrances. In ways unknown to me, the Psalms situate me in life, in the present moment, to live it fully for God. Slowly, as I begin to recognize that treasure in myself, I discern it shaping the lives of others too.

The language that the Psalms offer, however, goes yet another step further. The Psalms give a language for community. In singing the Psalms in worship, in singing them together, the community forms a heightened attentiveness to one another and to those around it, near and far. Verses in the Psalms refer to situations they have not experienced, but in this prayer, all those who have suffered these situations become sisters and brothers, neighbors. The community prays with them and knows itself to be one with them in a communion of prayer.

> The Psalms situate me in life, in the present moment, to live it fully for God.

This language, grounded in God's word, in the prayer of Jesus, marks the faith community. This Psalter becomes the language the community uses to define itself, to dialogue within its boundaries, to interpret the world around it, and to set out beyond those boundaries in service to the neighbor. Perhaps this new language—these words and works—is seen by those outside as naive or as a powerless means, and yet, through this powerlessness, the Holy Spirit crumbles walls of division.

The Psalms of course are but one part of communal prayer. The other part consists in prayer per se, intercessory prayer. There is a double movement in this pattern. On one side is psalmody, where God, like a parent, teaches the community how to pray, gives the community a language to speak to God, to the other, and to one's self. The Psalms immerse the community into the reality of Jesus Christ. The other side is intercessory prayer, an ardent prayer for the world, for those outside the circle of the community, beyond the walls of its immediate and internal concerns. Yes, intercessory prayer is for the community and its needs, but it is primarily for the neighbor, for the one crying out in the street. Intercessory prayer is like opening the windows of the sanctuary or church to let the call of the neighbor enter. Intercessory prayer brings into the midst of the community the suffering of the world by naming it. Once suffering has been named and brought to God, the community can no longer look on that suffering and turn away. The prayer forms it in an attentiveness to the world, in a responsibility and service to the world.

This double movement marks communal prayer: immersion in God's word (the Psalms) and ardent prayer for the world. God and neighbor are at the center of this journey of faith. Luther's own simple definition of Christian freedom applied to worship reflects this double movement: "For the glory of God and for the good of our neighbor and not for our own advantage and pleasure."[29]

6

Patterns Interrupted

Turning toward God and Neighbor

As this reflection comes to its conclusion, it is good perhaps to repeat and, in repeating, broaden what has been written. At the heart of prayer, the community is addressed and shaped by God and neighbor. Both are present in and with the community, calling it beyond the places, the contexts, where it wishes to remain. In this double movement—immersion in God's word (the Psalms) and an ardent prayer for the world—the community and every individual discovers a spirituality that is received, one that arises from the gift of faith itself. Common prayer takes on different forms throughout the centuries, but at its core is this double movement: the community turned toward God and neighbor.

Though I spent much time in the last chapter examining the dynamics of communal prayer, much remains to be explored.

Communal prayer in the churches in East Germany, especially in the 1980s, was diverse in form. The diversity was sometimes as wide as the number of groups hosting these prayers. In other words, one cannot look back to these prayer groups in Leipzig, just as one cannot look back at the early church or to the sixteenth century, to find one perfect model for communal prayer (or for Sunday worship, for that matter) for today. The same holds true for any cultural form of prayers—for example, those forms and style of music that were exported by Lutheran missionaries around the globe. Whether Norwegian, Swedish, German, or Finnish, those forms of prayers remain culturally embedded.

The singularity of origins—context and subjects—always should stand in the way of simple imitation. Scripture itself does not provide a particular model for worship, though it does describe patterns of prayers and ritual action that constitute worship. The danger of any model is one Luther warned about: human beings tend to take a particular model and turn it into a law. In other words, the liturgy calls for translation into every new context. However, the absence of a one-size-fits-all model does not mean anything goes. The worshipping community is presented with a challenge: living into that movement toward God and neighbor in such a way that the gospel is always translated and embodied today.

This gospel challenge does not ignore or dismiss the past, nor is it enslaved to it. In the prophet Isaiah it is written,

> Do not remember the former things,
> or consider the things of old.

I am about to do a new thing;

now it springs forth, do you not perceive it?

I will make a way in the wilderness

and rivers in the desert.

The wild animals will honor me,

the jackals and the ostriches;

for I give water in the wilderness,

rivers in the desert,

to give drink to my chosen people,

the people whom I formed for myself

so that they might declare my praise. (Isa 43:18–21)

God speaks about making all things new, but when God describes what this might be, God does so in terms of the old. The new thing, the thing that God does today, is what God always has done in the past: making a way through the wilderness. The challenge of communal prayer (and all liturgy) is to say the new with the old.

A worshipping community does not repeat rites received from the tradition simply because they are traditional. It examines the teaching (gospel) behind the rites. Do the rites introduce, teach, and welcome all into the gospel, the Christ event, death and resurrection? Do the rites translate the gospel as God's work in the midst of the world?

In the former East Germany, there were several forms of communal prayer. I have mentioned one that happened consistently throughout the decades: clandestine prayer groups, which began meeting in the crypt of the Berlin Cathedral in the 1950s. These small prayer groups served as a backdrop or backbone for other prayer groups that surfaced more officially in the 1980s.

The other, more public prayer groups were lodged in a few grassroots gatherings (*Basisgruppen*). These grassroots groups centered on three main themes: groups for peace (*Friedensgruppen*), environmental groups (*Umwelt Gruppen*), and human-rights groups (*Menschenrechtgruppen*). Of course, among these groups were many nonbelievers as well, and quite often, as former bishop of Thüringen Werner Leich shared, even nonbelievers participated in planning these prayers.[1]

The prayers, especially in the early 1980s, had something very spontaneous, even chaotic, about them. They served primarily as a means of expression: a chance to name what was ailing the world, the society, and the participants. In the context of the prayers, they could name what burdened them, and they exercised themselves in listening to the other.

> The prayers, especially in the early 1980s, had something very spontaneous, even chaotic, about them.

One of the prayers, a vesper service organized by the group Women for Peace, brought together various slides on the theme of women in the church. Each slide was accompanied by a prayer and then a meditation text, with occasional musical interludes. The entire service ended with a concluding prayer (taken from Mother Teresa), the Lord's Prayer, and a blessing. Not all the prayers were as well structured, as Pastor Groeger noted. "The prayers weren't always well thought out. They were all over the map!" But he added that this was also understandable, as these prayers "were the only form that people had to express their views, opinions."

Many pastors employed a hands-off strategy. They opened a space for such prayers to happen, a space where the people, especially the young people, knew they were safe. This is note-worthy in itself. At the outset, these prayers fumbled along through trial and error. Pastor Christopher Wonneberger of Dresden also noted this phenomenon. Pastor Wonneberger has come to be regarded as one of the principal mentors and leaders of these prayer groups, providing insight, stimulus, and courage throughout the 1980s. He took risks that gave shape to the prayers and the eventual manifestations on Monday evenings. He himself, though, could not participate in the final days as the wall came down, for he was suddenly debilitated by a major aneurysm.

In Dresden, where Pastor Wonneberger served in the early 1980s, there were many small prayer groups spread throughout the city. As he told me, the form of prayer was to be something free. "I didn't use a particular form. . . . I had more of an orienta-tion towards—I'll name it meditation—but even then it wasn't set. The philosopher Bloch wrote somewhere: 'The forms are for me more like a literary form, adaptable to where it needs to go.' Personally, I always adapt. Many others are more strict or even pietistic." For Pastor Wonneberger, liturgy was necessary as a means of gathering people, but then it was equally important to be free with the form, to interrupt. This freedom maintained a fine balance between form and improvisation.

For his theology diploma, Pastor Wonneberger had written on Bonhoeffer and what worship is to be in a nonreligious situation: "Lament and protest are bound together. Resistance and foresight, submission and resistance: we always need the two and we have to ask what is the most important *in this moment*. One must have a sense, "feel," the stage that one is in: Where are the ripe fruits? Which ones can be picked? One has to live with such things in order to reach others. Yes, submission also is important, because if you waste all your energies, you lose them. Submission is a time for renewal." The prayer that gathered people together was to be, in its very structure, a reflection of that intense listening, that active engagement in the life of society and this retreat, this stepping back. Only with active listening (vigilance) can one look forward, having a perspective beyond the present moment, and at the same time offer resistance. Prayer holds these together: resistance and submission, resistance and vigilance.

> Prayer holds these together: resistance and submission, resistance and vigilance.

These were not just words or a thesis for Pastor Wonneberger. He engaged with the society he lived in. For example, he turned to the world of East German literature:

> Reiner Kunze was really important because his writing was so lyrical and yet so quiet. I would hold little gatherings where we would read his texts. Once he came to one of our gatherings incognito. I did a lot of these things.

I always sought out those in the neighborhood whose voice wasn't heard, and invited them to the church and gave them voice. *Kirche fuer die Stimmloesse* [church for those without voice]: the church was to be a podium for those who couldn't raise their voice. I called these gatherings *Offene Lese Buehne* (open reading stage): Whoever wanted could come and read what they had. I did this a couple of times a year. Whoever came would find a forum.[2]

In these simple but daring and dangerous ways, Pastor Wonneberger and his parish listened to the street. They brought into the church the aspirations, the beauty, and the ugliness of the street. They also made space for the totally unexpected. But this is, according to Pastor Wonneberger, what the Easter Vigil teaches us. Celebrating life in the midst of darkness, one experiences life in its fullest. "The night shall be as bright as day, dazzling is the night for me, and full of gladness. The sanctifying power of this night dispels wickedness, washes faults away, restores innocence to the fallen, and joy to mourners, drives out hatred, fosters concord, and brings down the mighty" (Easter Exultet).

Martin Henker was a pastor in Meissen in the mid-1980s; later he became superintendent in Leipzig. He recalls,

Nineteen eighty-five—forty years after the end of the war. We organized a *Kreuzweg* [a procession of the cross]. We got this idea and started organizing it. The young people processed with the cross to different places in

the city: to places of injustice, to places that had something to do with atrocities of the war. We held a prayer
at each place, and this all culminated in a Eucharist in
the cathedral. The young people prepared a lot of this.
There was a cross that two people had to carry throughout the city from place to place. Because of the visibility,
the procession became like a demonstration. There was
a strong debate about this, and at the following year's
Good Friday, we were strongly pressured by the state: if
you do it again, you will be arrested. We hadn't asked for
permission the first time; we just did it.[3]

Some in the church tried to dissuade the young people from
processing again the following year, saying that the cross was too
precious to be used in public. But the young people got upset
at this suggestion. This procession and the acknowledgment of
solidarity with all those who have and are suffering, witnessing to this communion—this fellowship in the suffering of the
neighbor was for them of great spiritual importance.[4]

This particular prayer in Meissen took on a walking form.
As would be the case later in Leipzig, rather than processing to
the altar, the young people processed into the world to name
those places of intolerance, oppression, violence, and hatred. At
the end of the procession, they all gathered for a celebration of
the Eucharist in the cathedral. In the words of Pastor Henker,
"For the young people, the Eucharist was connected to a deep
sense of community. They were very much alone, solitary, in
their classrooms, etc., and the celebration of Holy Communion

brought them together. You will see an increase in the number of Eucharistic celebrations in our churches in the 1980s, and I think this is because of the young people. I still meet people who speak to me about the celebration of Holy Communion in the Meissen Cathedral at the end of these processions."

For Pastor Henker and the young people in Meissen, communal prayer was about the public act of confessing the faith (*Bekenntnis*): "We resist that the [Socialist] Party has a say over us and who we are. But we engage this confession through a deep trust in God." All of these prayers, whether in Dresden, Meissen, or Leipzig, were deeply connected to the street. The doors of the church were open to all. The young people went out into the street. This is what lies at the heart of psalmody and prayer, this double movement of faith that turns to God in praise and to the street in prayer, that turns to God in prayers and in praise engages the street.

In Leipzig, the more public prayers had varying degrees of impact throughout the 1980s. During the mid-1980s, the prayers for peace even dwindled down to merely three or four participants. Pastor Friedrich Magirius, superintendent of Leipzig-East and the one responsible for the St. Nicholas Church that hosted the prayers, insisted that the prayers continue. Pastor Henker commented that he did so "because [Magirius] thought that somewhere in this city, prayer had to continue. This was when the prayers were still prayers and not so much protests."[5]

As attendance began again to increase, the prayers were given a more structured character, a form that was welcoming to nonbelievers as well.[6] As mentioned, the prayer began with a greeting and then almost always the same songs: "We Shall Overcome" and *"Sonne der Gerechtigkeit"* or various Taizé songs, and often Psalm 85. Then came announcements, which played a central role. Here was a moment to listen to the street. No one knew what would be said, though most announcements focused on issues of the day, around the world, but also concerns at home, people who had been arrested or from whom nothing had been heard. As noted in the text *Prayers and Peace*, "We had to improvise because news was often quite fresh."[7] There was usually a very short homily and then extensive prayers, often with a sung kyrie from Taizé. In some cases, there was space in the chancel area for many little candles and people were invited to formulate prayers and bring their candles to that area. At other times, different groups were invited to share their concerns and other issues after the prayers, rather than before or during the announcements. The Lord's Prayer was prayed, a blessing was spoken, and perhaps another hymn was sung, often *"Komm Herr Segne Uns."* Then people went out into the streets with their lighted candles. Selah.

Prayer Shaped by the Neighbor

Communal prayer is an expression of what I have called a baptismal spirituality or baptismal discipline. The shaping of life through faith by the Holy Spirit takes on a communal form. This communal dimension came more and more into focus through that unique fellowship discovered in baptism (not just in Christ, but with the neighbor) and through the realization that in the depth of prayer, I am not alone; there is always another, Jesus Christ (and the whole communion of saints).

This fellowship becomes visible. It became visible in the small prayer groups in East Germany, when two or three, four or five, or many were shaped by something from God ("Where two or three are gathered . . ."). Communal prayer is a place of this shaping by the Holy Spirit. The Psalms, at the heart of communal prayer, immerse the community into the communion of saints. The Psalms keep the community and all participants in that communion because they share and shape the community in the joy, fear, hope, and sadness of the saints.[8]

The shaping of community through prayer by the Holy Spirit is also an unexpected shaping by the neighbor, by the ones named in the prayer, and by the uncontrollable cries, concerns, anguish, hopes, and longings of the neighbor, including (and especially) the unfamiliar neighbors who are not part of the community. Communal prayer renders the community vulnerable to the working of the Holy Spirit outside its walls and its established customs, language, and values.

> Communal prayer renders the community vulnerable to the working of the Holy Spirit outside its walls.

This alternation of contemplation and prayer with solidarity is nothing new in the history of Christian communities. Many of the prayer groups in former East Germany were inspired by the community of Taizé in

France, which embodies in its life what Brother Roger called "contemplation and struggle." As already shown, the pattern of psalmody and prayer actualizes a theological grammar: life immersed in God's word and human solidarity. Faith itself is exercised both in praise and in lament, in joyful response and in struggle, in silence and in encounter.

As you will recall, the Psalms are an external word addressed to us. This word, this language, becomes that of the community through the prayer, through silence and gesture and supplication. There are many different genres of texts among the Psalms. There are psalms praising human beings who are upright in the way of the Lord. There are psalms that reflect on the way of the just as compared to the way of the wicked. There are psalms that describe God's action in history, through exodus and exile and God's work in creation. There are psalms that address and give instructions to the anointed one, the king. There are psalms that condemn the evil one. There are psalms that describe human suffering, a suffering that may be completely out of the experience of the praying community, and yet there they are, in solidarity with extreme anguish.

The Psalms reveal not just the works and words but the very heart of a dialogue—known or unknown—the very heart of an encounter with the living God. In the Psalms, the community is held in this dialogue. In a fervent intercessory prayer, the doors and windows of the sanctuary are opened to the street, to the neighborhood, to the world. The praying community is opened up to a vision and a hope and a commitment to justice.

Communal prayer is a place, a particular dynamic that exercises faith. "This common prayer," Luther writes, "is precious and the most effective, and it is for the sake of this that we assemble ourselves together. The church is called a house of prayer because we are all there as a congregation and with one accord to bring our own needs as well as those of all [people] before God and to call upon [God] for mercy."⁹ This intercessory prayer, exercising faith, opens the community up toward a fellowship with one another and with the neighbor, for the world.

Living the Partial

This spirituality received and exercised in communal prayer is, of course, first embodied quite literally in the act of baptism, which sets one on a new way, in new creation. Prayer is in fact a language, an act, an event, an utterance that continually trains me to apprehend, to see, to recognize the hidden way that God is tracing throughout history. Prayer, like the *selah* of the Psalms, interrupts my usual rhythms to focus me on a gospel rhythm.

Selah has been somewhat of a leitmotif throughout this writing. As a word uttered in the Psalms, as a word uttered by Pastor Groeger in the telling of events too difficult to put into words, it points to that hidden way. *Selah* interrupts the poetic flow and signals, over and over, a silence at the heart of prayer, at the heart of life, at the heart of history, at the heart of creation. A mystery resides at the heart, a singular event, which I've called originary, in that one knows it only as it becomes over and over, as it originates over and over, in the present moment, in this place, now. An utterance resonates throughout history and throughout the life of individuals and communities, but it is a silent utterance (Ps 19). History is marked by something latent.

Selah interrupts the poetic flow and signals, over and over, a silence at the heart of prayer.

The Spirit's utterance permeates life. Paradoxically, it utters, it announces an absent thing, something latent, something not immediately seen or heard or experienced. The words of the Spirit announce an absent thing only apprehended by faith.[10] God's mode of operation appears to be as absence or latency, or as a contrary thing. Yet, throughout history, throughout each life, the Spirit weaves a way deeper than anyone could ever imagine on their own into God's reclaiming and reconciling action, ever deeper into righteousness, into gospel.

In the sentence "The words of the Spirit announce an absent thing," Luther suggests more than just the hidden plan of God permeating history. The absent thing also points to a fundamental condition of life. The absent thing that the Spirit announces is the radical provisionality of life, or, in the words of the mystics, the incompleteness or the partial quality of life. In this life, I will see or know or live only in part (1 Cor 13:9). There always will be a hole: a missing piece, an empty space, selah, in every event, in every context, in every heart throughout history. But this missing piece—that absent thing, an inherent latency—opens a way.

Luther was deeply influenced by German mysticism. He studied it well. At the same time he sought to define God's righteousness, a year before publishing the *Ninety-Five Theses*, he edited and published in 1516 an extremely influential piece of literature from the mystical tradition, *Theologia Deutsch (A German Theology)*.[11] Luther was the first, in fact, to have rendered this text public, and he considered it one of the most important books he had ever read.

The opening chapter of *Theologia Deutsch* is a reflection on the whole and the partial, or the complete and the incomplete, citing Paul in 1 Corinthians 13. With simple words, the unknown author states, "And all the partial things is not the complete thing."[12] All creaturely things, all things, events, persons of this life—even put all together—are not the fulfillment of life. It is a simple insight, but it holds one of the keys, I believe, to understanding spirituality. This little insight highlights that fundamental condition of life: all human striving, especially the striving for God, will remain unfulfilled. The created order, though good, is not perfect.[13] Desire will never meet its object. History will never hold the answer to its own meaning. Life will not be found in an existential centering.

Desire, the need for fulfillment, does not define who I am as a human being. When I (mistakenly) think it does, I turn many objects of this life into little gods. Then, even my spiritual quest, my holiest inclination, my best works of charity, become idolatrous. The *Theologia Deutsch* states, along with Paul, that the context, the landscape I create for my life, no matter how beautifully or perfectly constructed, is always only just half the picture. There is another landscape, another field, one whose boundaries mark a place of delight (Ps 16). This field is faith.

Faith establishes a field in which I experience life to the fullest, even in a world of partial knowledge, of dim perception, of half-moons. This is not contradictory, for in faith a person is given all things. Jesus says, "Truly I tell you, there is no one who has left house or brothers or sisters or mother or father or children or fields for my sake and for the sake of the good news, who will not receive a hundredfold now in this age—houses, brothers and sisters, mothers and children, and fields with persecutions—and in the age to come eternal life" (Mark 10:29–30). There is no need to move beyond the partial in order to find fullness, no need to move out of this world into a heavenly realm. Rather, the movement is ever deeper into the life that has been given. In faith, all things are experienced without the compulsion of possession or the self-centered preoccupation of hoarding, without the worry of making them carry more meaning than they can or turning them into something absolute.

I cannot of course know the wholeness that is God. It is an absent thing uttered by the Holy Spirit. However, in the *Theologia Deutsch*, as then in Luther, this fullness can be recognized, sensed, and tasted.[14] Its sweetness draws me in. Curiously, the *Theologia Deutsch* does not ask "What is the fullness of God, and how do I know it?" Rather, it asks "When does it come?" With this question, the action of knowing as conceptual representation or appropriation of an object is displaced. Instead of cognitively knowing, there is simply an encounter with one who comes. All else (including all knowledge) flows from this encounter.

Words fail to describe this unsayable experientia. I experience with my whole body—intellectually, emotionally, sensually. But these movements of the heart never become the subject, the center. The sweetness of God's fullness always remains the subject, which creates a space around itself and is apprehended by faith. Blessed are the ones who walk in this way, in the way of righteousness, like trees planted by streams of living water; they too give sweet fruit.

Luther's mysticism replaces the mystics' preoccupation with a journey to another place, to a heavenly height, to a lost homeland, whether in the past or in the future. Yes, Luther still uses the metaphor of journey, as I have shown, but journey is a movement not toward something in another time and space, but a movement ever deeper into the field that God has marked out for me, for this community, and always in this moment. When Luther writes about the journey into righteousness in his *Disputation on Justification* (1534), this journey is a heightening and deepening, an intensification within life of God's unconditional promise, of reconciliation what has already arrived.

This intensification of righteousness always includes the community and the neighbor: living today for God and the neighbor. My life is only life as it is created, dies, and rises with those around me, in community. Psalm 1 reminds me of this community. The blessed live in a community (Ps 1:5). Those who walk on this hidden way are in community. Faith is communal. Faith pushes me always to the other, not as an object of desire, but as a subject who is Christ; not as desire, but as communion; not as an ethical imperative, but as a gift; not as work, but already reconciled. Faith is marked by a profound reconciliation, because I no longer have to justify myself but simply serve one another.[15]

A profound reconciliation—peace—characterizes this hidden way known fully only by God and revealed by God's Spirit. Latent within history, the community is called in faith to an attentiveness, a vigilance, a patience, and a hope as it discerns and encourages all signs of such reconciliation and peace in the messiness of everyday life and in the more often tumultuous and worrisome trends in society, the nation, and the world. This gospel reality—the reality, in fact, of the Sermon on the Mount (Matt 5), where the enemy is no longer an enemy but perceived as a partner, neighbor[16]—when discerned, is like a summer thundershower, washing the old away and making everything new, crumbling walls, and destroying barriers. Vigil candles silence tanks.

> Faith is communal. Faith pushes me always to the other.

I have named this washing and new creation a baptismal spirituality. It may be likened to a *via negativa*. It is characterized by a deconstruction. All the hindrances I establish in and around myself are either whittled away or outright torn down by the

Spirit. There is an "eradication of blocks," as Jerzy Grotowski writes.[17] But this eradication does not put the individual on a special, personal, mystical path to union with God in the heavenly heights. Faith is deconstruction rooted in God's unconditional promise: No wall, no barrier, can separate me from that love. Nothing. Only faith.

Only faith reveals the absent thing that circumscribes life in marvelous ways, for God penetrates the way of the just, Psalm 1 declares. The fullness of life permeates, inundates, the deepest recesses of those who walk on this hidden way. God as absence is experienced as fullness in this life, through faith. This absence/fullness sensed, touched, and tasted then also sustains faith. Because I do not yet know fully, but only in part, because this absent thing continually returns, faith springs forth from weary hearts. God's absence calls to my own incompleteness. Deep calls to deep (Ps 42), and in those depths, a silent thanksgiving—eucharistia—arises. Prayer. Selah.

Silence

The landscape of faith stretches over all of life, touching all corners of existence. Faith is known, to a degree, by the constant struggle that it provokes in everyday life. The daily dying and rising I experience, the confrontation and rebirth I undergo, this experientia forms the heart: it formed the people in Leipzig participating in the prayer groups, and it forms you and me as spiritual beings where the spiritual is not divided from the physical, from the messiness of life. In Leipzig, in the worshipping community, the struggle was felt deeply even and especially as all was changing. Pastor Groeger remarked, "You can't believe the fear we had on October 9 [1989]."[18]

The eleventh-century Easter sequence *Victimae Paschali* might help contextualize this confrontation and struggle: "*Mors et vita duello / conflixere mirando: / dux vitae mortuus, / regnat vivus*" (Death and life contended in a spectacular battle: the Prince of life, who died, yet reigns alive!). Luther wrote an Easter hymn on the same text: "*Es war ein wunderlicher Krieg, Da Tod und Leben rungen, Das Leben behielt den Sieg. . . . Es hat den Tod verschlungen*" (It was a strange battle where death and life struggled. Life won the victory; it has swallowed up death).

The struggle is finally one between life and death, between a world closed in on myself and one that is open up to the world, all of creation, the neighbor, and God. One world is curved in on itself; the other is welcome, arms opened in generosity. Luther translates the Latin *mirando* (marvelous) with *wunderlicher* (extraordinary, wonderful), which highlights how strange, even confusing and odd, this struggle is. The struggle is not between two equal forces. A Christian cosmology rooted in Paul (and later Augustine) knows only one God, one power that is all-loving and good. It is, according to Paul, an ongoing cosmic battle in which God is reclaiming the cosmos, step by step. It is a battle that began with the victory at the cross so beautifully described by St. John Chrysostom in his Easter sermon (ca. 400 CE): "Hell is in an uproar, for it is now made captive. Hell took a body, and discovered God. It took earth, and encountered Heaven. It took what it saw, and was overcome by what it did not see."[19]

In the midst of this struggle, I am often more aware of its strangeness and the confusion it creates. The struggle is always one with limits. It is a double-sided struggle. On the one hand, my ego seeks that which is beyond the boundaries set by faith—you shall have no other gods. I keep looking for other gods. I want to transgress this first commandment and find more immediate fulfillment and satisfaction in things and people and situations. Transgression takes the form of illusion as well, when I imagine (or convince myself) that all these other gods (objects of my desire or love) are perfectly compatible with belief in a supreme god.

In prayer, in the community, I become more and more attuned to this struggle deep within human history, at the heart of the cosmos. The struggle affects all areas of existence, conscious and unconscious, rational and erotic. Language fails to capture or comprehend or communicate this *experientia*. This strange struggle must find words from elsewhere. Words need to be borrowed—from the Psalms, for example. In the heart of prayer, I am still taught how to pray. What other language is available?

Between the dying and the rising, between the deconstruction and the new creation, is a hiatus, an abyss, a pit. Holy Saturday stands between Good Friday and the Easter Vigil. It is the middle day.[20] Christ descends to the dead. A silence hovers over all creation. In this silence, in speechlessness—that is, in faith—a world unfolds that the Holy Spirit is creating not only in me or for me, but as a communion with the neighbor, for the other, with all creation. Selah.

Silence is a language offered to the community, though it is a language from which most people flee. Instead of silence, spaces are filled with images and sounds. Time is filled with activities. This is true even in worship, in communal prayer. The flight from silence takes form in endless words from prayers to sermons. Luther is quick to condemn those who shuffle papers and say many prayers in church.[21] Those who engage in such activities can too quickly find that they are praising themselves and not God.

Words are valuable, but in a strange way they are simply stepping stones training one to be without words. One should hold on to words and pray them for as long as it takes for wings to grow, so that one can fly without words.[22] Words carry in themselves the danger of becoming merely self-centered praise. All language is on some level a sacrifice. Silence, however, brings one to a right understanding of the words. That is, silence disrupts the filters of the ego (both interpretation and praise) and reveals the vulnerability of the heart, out of which perhaps a new language, a new grammar, can be formulated.

> Silence, however, brings one to a right understanding of the words.

Luther is careful to point out that he does not reject prayers spoken out loud, nor the use of words, for words are a great gift of God.[23] In An Exposition of the Lord's Prayer (*Auslegung des*

Vaterunsers, 1519), he underlines this fact: words are not to be thrown out, and one is to be always attentive to their use. If they are not spoken in order to move hearts, then they should be discarded.[24] Words are meant to move the heart to silence. Words are meant to move the heart to faith.

I will confess that I suffer when words are used aggressively in worship. Such use or overuse of words leads to muteness and disengagement rather than silence. The Enlightenment and the "modern man" is still alive and well when the doctrine of justification by faith alone is proclaimed as a rational (and purely audible) truth, when a forensic framing of justification reduces it to an audible pronouncement, or when the heart is objectified and the pastor or priest appears more as a clinician (or even judge) than a servant. Curiously, such an approach to justification verges on what Luther struggled to avoid: the magical, as if by the mere pronouncement of the words something happens.

Justification, however, defines a unique relationship with God. Again, in An Exposition of the Lord's Prayer, Luther reflects on the first verse, "Our Father in heaven." He lays special value on the contradiction inherent in that verse: the believer calls God "Father," but God is inaccessible (in heaven). Yet, Luther argues, if Christ has taught his followers this prayer, it is because, through Christ, everyone has access to God the Father in heaven. Through Christ, this loving parental relationship is established. The Lord's Prayer not only affirms the truth of the relationship that justifies and reconciles, but makes this relationship a reality, something existential, even if I do not understand what all the words of the prayer mean. In fact, it is even better,

Luther notes, that one does not understand, for then the heart speaks more than the words.[25]

Words are to be rooted in silence. They spring forth out of that silence defined by God, who marks the pleasant boundaries for the community.

The wonderful field circumscribed by God's command, engendering faith, reveals that silence at the heart of life. Perhaps one of the greatest challenges every person faces is simply living in this silence. "Be still, and know that I am God" (Ps 46:10). Those who strive after many things, who always seek the latest fad, whether commercial or spiritual, don't hear the voice in the wilderness, the cry in the street. They are afraid to be quiet and rest, to be silent. They are, Luther writes in his commentary on the first psalm, like Saul, who could not be silent or rest but kept striving to self-justify and fulfill hisself.

Silence is both the beginning and the end of prayer. Silence is not passive, nor is it simply introspection. God establishes this justifying, reconciling, complete relationship in silence—in the deadening silence of Good Friday, in the disarming silence of Holy Saturday, and in the astounding proclamation of Easter Sunday, whose words reach to the ends of the universe, though no voice is heard.

> The heavens are telling the glory of God;
>> and the firmament proclaims God's handiwork.
> Day to day pours forth speech,
>> and night to night declares knowledge.
> There is no speech, nor are there words;
>> their voice is not heard;

yet their voice goes out through all the earth,
and their words to the end of the world. (Ps 19:1–4)

Silence is listening to these voiceless words, vigilant and patient. In silence, I become attentive to all that surrounds me, and to the voiceless, the suffering, the marginalized. Silence characterizes a life of faith. It belongs to a Christian, Luther writes, especially one who wants to pray and praise, to be patient, to be silent. "Therefore it is said, praise God in silence—that means that we are not impatient, but that we learn to linger and be vigilant and continue in faith."[26]

Silence is not a reality above and beyond everyday life, nor a state to which I aspire by extracting myself from the messiness of the world. Silence is not a realm of repose or a sort of existential oblivion. Luther defines silence in words that speak about one's relationship to God. One is to listen, to be patient, to learn, and to wait. The Holy Spirit prays within each person far more than they can imagine, often only as a whisper. This silence is inhabited by the other, by Christ, and by the neighbor. In silence, God and neighbor, Jesus Christ, become truly one with me.

> In silence, God and neighbor, Jesus Christ, become truly with me.

Those who flee the silence, the impatient, cut themselves off from such a relationship with God. The impatient believe that God is not acting as God should—that is, as they would like God to act. But perhaps we often all are such impatient ones who know better what is needed both for us and for others. Impatience limits God, fitting God into my timetable. Luther writes that the impatient "hurt themselves because they no longer can pray or sing praise."[27] I hurt myself, the community hurts itself, when I lose the proper perspective on my life and its place in the world in relationship to God. By refusing prayer and praise, I cut myself off from God and neighbor. I end up living in my own narrow constructions and in self-justification.

Justification by faith alone, before it is a doctrine or a theological paradigm, is the silence of all creation before God. It is the awareness of the partial, the incomplete. It is the deep recognition that, in the end, I have nothing but what God has given: faith. I have only faith. Faith defines life and gives all that is needed within the partial, the incomplete—and in that realization, I am already on that hidden way that the Holy Spirit is tracing throughout history, reconciling all things to God's self: God's way.

In prayer and praise, the worshipping community is brought to the outermost edge of the communicable. It discovers that its first language is silence. "*Tibi silentium, laus*" (For you, silence is praise, O God, in Zion), sings Psalm 65:1 in the Vulgate that Luther used and in certain modern translations.[28] Praise is not only joyful exuberance, but perhaps first of all a silence that is an expression of faith. It is an utter dependence that breaks opens all other dependencies—all other walls, barriers, desires, and idols—and sets the community on a new, hidden way. Selah.

POSTLUDE:
PRAYER IN A TIME OF PHYSICAL DISTANCING

This book was being completed as the world was beginning to shut down because of COVID-19. I'm grateful that the editors have allowed me to add a postlude reflecting on the current situation through daily prayer.

The simple structure of daily prayer—psalmody, silence, prayer—holds the faith community through both good times and difficult times, times of thanksgiving and times of lament, times of togetherness and times of separation. In this time of pandemic, communities find themselves once again behind closed doors, unable to meet physically together in one space.

Like the underground prayer groups, no more than a few people may gather together today, but unlike the underground prayer groups, connectivity is enabled online. Or is it really a different situation? A connectivity occurs in communal prayer that is not defined by seeing faces on a screen or hearing each other read or sing. Such connectivity occurs through the Holy Spirit who forges a communion deep through our bodies, through our whole existence, through our hearts. Those who participated in the underground prayer groups embodied the communion of saints. Though many groups never "met," they knew each other in a unique way, beyond either the physical or the virtual gathering.

Virtual reality carries emotions, various states of being, many expressions, and enables a group to be together in times of restraint and physical distancing when the body of Christ cannot meet physically but gathers in many different places. It renders tangible a connectivity that faith and prayer have already established. Praying online, whether live-streamed or pre-recorded, heightens an awareness of a depth of communion that constitutes human reality. It does not create that communion.

The Holy Spirit creates new affections deep in the heart. The psalms shape and nurture, water, tend, and cultivate these affections. God creates anew and continually from and in the midst of the many different situations in which humanity finds itself. The faith community, living and witnessing to new creation, brings its struggle to God, pleading with God, to strengthen it and to open hearts to a new way. Prayer is not for a return to the "normal" but a leap into God's future.

Intercessory prayer in a time of pandemic names the context, the suffering, the injustice, and the hope. Perhaps the faith community in prayer begins by naming the turmoil and burden of illness and fear in which humanity lives, the confusion and anxiety created by COVID-19. Of course, the prayer calls for healing and protection from the coronavirus; the community seeks strength to live in self-discipline for the good of the neighbor and also healing from self-centeredness and indifference.

The community also names the many other diseases from which the world suffers, and that claim so many lives, often unnoticed to the vast majority: malaria, dengue fever, HIV and AIDS.

The prayer pleads for strength and courage for all those in public health services and for inspiration for researchers and scientists. The community, in its prayer, asks that government leaders may speak the truth, halt the spread of misinformation, and act with justice so that the whole human family may know healing.

The prayer also pleads for protection and support for those caught at home in abusive relationships, for those suffering from gender-based violence, for all those without a home to find shelter, for those without health care, for refugees and displaced persons who lack running water or the ability to protect themselves. for the respect of human rights, for all who have been created in God's image. "May God's original intention be restored."[1] The prayer intercedes as well as for those who have lost work, businesses, and livelihoods. It names its solidarity with those who, even without the pandemic, are not able to regularly join the worshipping community because of age, debilitating illness, or other various mental and physical challenges. And it entrusts to God's gentle embrace all those who have died or will die this day.

Of course, this list is never complete. Intercessory prayer pushes us to hear the cry within the community and to open the door to hear the cry of the neighbor in their fear and suffering. The faith community can step into that suffering, into that human reality, because it has been shaped by faith through the encounter of God's Word in Scripture and in particular through the psalms. Of course, in this time of pandemic, the community's service takes on many different forms that respect the need of distance in order to abet the spread of the virus, but its prayer is always outwardly focused and continually shaping the community's imagination and love for our neighbor.

Psalmody, silence, and prayer heighten within the community a sense of vigilance and attentiveness. In a COVID-19 world, a world that will not end with the end of an immediate threat of the coronavirus, the faith community is invited into something different. God invites it into the space of human finitude. God invites faith communities to enter into another dimension of the communion of saints—a yearning that is rooted in faith.

Perhaps the gospel today is about waiting and yearning in God. This yearning directs the community to the heart of "by faith alone," which is nothing but the experience of having everything stripped away to find oneself relying only on God through faith. In times of pandemic, faith communities are invited into this spiritual discipline of letting go, of abandonment, of restraint. God does not disappoint the waiting or searching heart, the waiting and yearning community. The yearning of faith—a communal yearning—also nurtures an expanded and growing dimension of communion within the human family. This yearning is a new spiritual reality for many, yet it is also an ancient one that characterizes the communion of saints, always sustained by daily prayer and action.

Dirk G. Lange
Pentecost 2020

NOTES

INTRODUCTION

1. John Paul II, "Message of His Holiness Pope John Paul II for the XXIX World Day of Peace," Vatican (January 1, 1996), https://tinyurl.com/v6csl9j.
2. Lutheran World Federation, "The Church in the Public Space: A Study Document of the Lutheran World Federation" (2016), https://tinyurl.com/uvss5hj.
3. Hans-Jürgen Sievers (pastor, Evangelical Reformed Church of Leipzig), interview by author (July 13, 2010).
4. Neues Forum Leipzig, ed., *Jetzt oder nie–Demokratie! Leipziger Herbst '89. Zeugnisse, Gespraeche, Dokumente* (Leipzig: Forum Verlag Leipzig, 1989), 49.
5. Martin Luther, *The Large Catechism*, in *BC* 381.
6. Sievers, interview.
7. *LW* 11 (on Ps 85:10).
8. Martin Luther, "On Rogationtide Prayer and Procession," *LW* 42:89.
9. Martin Luther, "Treatise on Good Works," *LW* 44:79–80.
10. Luther, "Treatise on Good Works," 79–80.
11. Dietrich Bonhoeffer, *Letters and Papers from Prison* (Minneapolis: Fortress, 2010), 389.
12. Sievers, interview.

CHAPTER 1: SPIRITUALITY

1. Ernest Becker, *The Denial of Death* (New York: Free Press, 1997), 153.
2. Dietrich Bonhoeffer, *Life Together* and *Prayerbook of the Bible* (Minneapolis: Fortress, 2005), 39.
3. Luther, *Large Catechism*, 386.
4. Dirk G. Lange, *Trauma Recalled: Liturgy, Disruption, Theology* (Minneapolis: Fortress, 2009), 141.
5. Bonhoeffer, *Letters and Papers from Prison*, 503.
6. Christoph Wonneberger (pastor), interview by author (July 17, 2010).
7. St. Thomas Church—the church of J. S. Bach and the St. Thomas Boys Choir (*Thomanerchor*)—did not fully participate until the penultimate days of the manifestations.
8. In the former East Germany, the Kirchentag was an independently organized yet regional gathering of Protestant Christians. Today in Germany, it is a significant, independent gathering of Protestant Christians occurring every two years.
9. Sievers, interview.
10. *Platzregen*—a summer thunderstorm that pours down heavily in one particular area and then passes by, allowing the sun to come out again!
11. Bonhoeffer, *Letters and Papers from Prison*, 280–81.
12. Erwin Mülhaupt, *D. Martin Luthers: Psalmen Auslegung, 1. Band Psalmen 1–25* (Göttingen: Vandenhoeck & Ruprecht, 1959), 13–14.
13. Ps 1:6: "For the Lord watches over the way of the righteous, but the way of the wicked will perish."
14. Mülhaupt, *Psalmen Auslegung*, 11.
15. For more on the affections, see Don E. Saliers, *The Soul in Paraphrase: Prayer and the Religious Affections*, 5th ed. (White Sulphur Springs, WV: OSL, 2015).
16. Augsburg Confession, article XX, in *BC* 57.
17. "The experience of trauma, the fact of latency, would thus seem to consist, not in the forgetting of a reality that can hence never be fully known, but in an inherent latency within the experience

itself." Cathy Caruth, *Unclaimed Experience: Trauma, Narrative, and History* (Baltimore: Johns Hopkins University Press, 1996), 17.

18. Even if the word *journey* has been overused and often wrongly understood, I will continue to use it and uncover new dimensions of this journey and add another metaphor to describe this way in the following chapters.

19. Birgit Stolt, *Martin Luther: Rhetorik des Herzen* (Stuttgart: Mohr Siebeck, 2000), 33.

20. Stolt, *Martin Luther*, 34.

21. See Luther's semiautobiographical sketch in his "Preface to the Latin Works," *LW* 34:325–38.

22. These are all words Luther uses to describe this knowing of the heart (see Stolt, *Martin Luther*, 36). See also Oswald Bayer, *Martin Luther's Theology: A Contemporary Interpretation*, trans. Thomas H. Trapp (Grand Rapids: Eerdmans, 2008), 35.

23. Malvasier is a sweet wine found today primarily in Spain.

24. Mülhaupt, *Psalmen Auslegung*, 20.

25. Mülhaupt, *Psalmen Auslegung*, 21.

26. Mülhaupt, *Psalmen Auslegung*, 3–4.

27. *WADB* 101:99–105.

28. Luther understands the Psalms christologically, as the prayerbook of a Christian community.

29. Mülhaupt, *Psalmen Auslegung*, 12.

30. Martin Luther, citing Ps 110:3 (Mülhaupt, *Psalmen Auslegung*, 8).

31. Bonhoeffer, *Letters and Papers from Prison*, 503.

32. See Deanne Thompson, *Crossing the Divide: Luther, Feminism and the Cross* (Minneapolis: Fortress, 2004). See also Marit Trelstad, ed., *Cross Examinations: Readings on the Meaning of the Cross Today* (Minneapolis: Fortress, 2006).

CHAPTER 2: TODAY EVERYTHING IS DIFFERENT

1. "*Herr Pfarrer, heute ist alles anderes.*" At this point in the narrative, Pastor Wolfgang Groeger had to stop and remain silent for some time. Wolfgang Groeger (pastor), interview with author, July 7, 2010.

2. *LW* 1:117.

3. *WA* 3:301, concerning Ps 53 (Hebrew Ps 54).

4. Heinrich Schlier, *Die Zeit der Kirche* (Freiburg: Herder, 1956), 273.

5. Matthias Claudius, "The Evening Song" (*"Der Mond is aufgegangen"*).

6. *Verba enim spiritus sunt annunciata de re absente et non apparente, per fidem apprehendenenda.* The words of the spirit announce an absent thing, not to be seen, but apprehended by faith. See *WA* 5:239.

7. Michel de Certeau, *The Practice of Everyday Life* (Berkeley: University of California Press, 2011), 1:33.

8. Judith Butler, *Gender Trouble: Feminism and the Subversion of Identity* (New York: Routledge, 2006).

9. De Certeau, *Practice of Everyday Life*, and a very helpful commentary by Ben Highmore, *Michel de Certeau: Analysing Culture* (London: Continuum, 2006), 108.

10. Dorothee Soelle, *The Silent Cry: Mysticism and Resistance* (Minneapolis: Fortress, 2001), 193.

11. Martin Luther, *Psalm 1 Aus der ersten Psalmenvorlesung* (1513/15), *WA* 5.

12. Mülhaupt, *Psalmen Auslegung,* 9.

13. *LW* 42:90; *WA* 2:178.

14. *LW* 42:91.

15. Charles Taylor, *A Secular Age* (Cambridge, MA: Belknap Press of Harvard University Press, 2007), 29.

16. *LW* 42:91.

17. Bonhoeffer, *Letters and Papers from Prison,* 364 (April 30, 1944).

18. Bonhoeffer, *Letters and Papers from Prison,* 360–61 (July 16, 1944). See also Larry L. Rasmussen, *Dietrich Bonhoeffer: Reality and Resistance* (Louisville: Westminster John Knox, 2005), 83.

19. Dietrich Bonhoeffer, *Discipleship* (Minneapolis: Fortress, 2003), 53–56.

20. *LW* 41:149–65. See also Gordon W. Lathrop and Timothy J. Wengert, *Christian Assembly: Marks of the Church in a Pluralistic Age* (Minneapolis: Fortress, 2004).

21. Rasmussen, *Dietrich Bonhoeffer*, 59, 76.
22. Bonhoeffer, *Letters and Papers from Prison*, 389.
23. Jerzy Grotowski, *Towards a Poor Theatre* (New York: Routledge, 2002), 17.
24. *LW* 27 (on Gal 2:19).

CHAPTER 3: FAITH AND PRAYER

1. Bonhoeffer, *Discipleship*, 43–56.
2. Mülhaupt, *Psalmen Auslegung*, 9. See also 1 Sam 15:22.
3. The two ways (as described in Chapter 1) consist of a way of faith and a way of unbelief, or a way of dependence on God and a way that relies only on human counsel.
4. Bonhoeffer, *Life Together*, 94.
5. Mülhaupt, *Psalmen Auslegung*, 9.
6. Martin Luther, "Disputation on Justification," *LW* 34:23.
7. See Flannery O'Connor, "Revelation," in *The Complete Short Stories* (New York: Farrar, Straus, & Giroux, 1971), 488–509.
8. Luther, "Disputation on Justification," 153.
9. *LW* 26:129–30.
10. *LW* 26 (on Gal 2:16).
11. *LW* 51:72.
12. *LW* 25:444.
13. *LW* 26 (on Gal 2:17).
14. *LW* 35:30.
15. Both Pastor Christoph Wonneberger and Pastor Wolfgang Groeger, independently of each other, attested to the struggle of finding a new impetus to the prayer without simply adding elements. They also attested to the fact that the prayers weren't always well planned or carried out.
16. For use of this phrase, see Glenn L. Borreson, "Bonhoeffer on Baptism: Discipline for the Sake of the Gospel," *Word & World* 1, no. 1 (1981): 20–31.
17. Bonhoeffer, *Discipleship*, 208.
18. Bonhoeffer, *Discipleship*, 210.
19. *LW* 41:161.

20. Bonhoeffer, *Letters and Papers from Prison*, 370.
21. Luther, *Large Catechism*, 381.
22. *LW* 44:67.
23. Joseph Herl, *Worship Wars in Early Lutheranism* (Oxford: Oxford University Press, 2004), 5.
24. Communal prayer was not meant to replace the Sunday celebration of word and sacrament.
25. See also Luther's insistence on the regularity of prayer in his letter to the Master Barber Peter (*LW* 43).
26. "This meditation [or prayer] transforms a person's being and, almost like baptism, gives a new birth. Here the passion of Christ performs its natural and noble work, strangling the old Adam and expelling all joy, delight, and confidence that a person could find in other creatures, even as Christ was forsaken by all, even by God." See Martin Luther, "Meditation on the Passion of Christ," *LW* 42:11.
27. Groeger, interview.
28. *BC* 441.
29. *LW* 44:80.
30. Contrary to Robert Jenson's assertion in "The Praying Animal," *Zygon* 18, no. 3 (September 1983): 311–25.
31. Bonhoeffer, *Prayerbook of the Bible*, 155.
32. Augsburg Confession, article XX, 57.
33. To name just two works from a multitude of art forms, past and present.
34. Luther, *Large Catechism*, 441.
35. *LW* 42:87.
36. See Luther on how the devil wishes people to read Scripture in this way, thus causing many factions and divisions among Christians (*LW* 37:13–14).
37. See Luther on how Origen brought the allegorical or spiritual meaning into interpretation, and how Paul makes a much finer distinction in his letter to the Galatians (*LW* 39:180).
38. *LW* 34:285.
39. *LW* 39:181.
40. *LW* 39:181.

41. *LW* 34:286.
42. Bayer, *Martin Luther's Theology*, 36.

CHAPTER 4: BAPTISMAL SPIRITUALITY

1. *WA* 5:163.
2. *WA* 3:372.
3. *WA* 5:497.
4. *LW* 44:31.
5. Caruth, *Unclaimed Experience*, 64, emphasis original.
6. Cathy Caruth, *Trauma: Explorations in Memory* (Baltimore: Johns Hopkins University Press, 1995), 151.
7. Michel de Certeau, *The Capture of Speech and Other Political Writings* (Minneapolis: University of Minnesota Press, 1997), 20.
8. De Certeau, *Capture of Speech*, 26.
9. *WA* 5:239.
10. Luther, *Large Catechism*, commentary on the first commandment, *BC* 386–92.
11. Mülhaupt, *Psalmen Auslegung*, 7, 10.
12. Mülhaupt, *Psalmen Auslegung*, 11.
13. Mülhaupt, *Psalmen Auslegung*, 16.
14. Mülhaupt, *Psalmen Auslegung*, 15.
15. *LW* 54:xvii; Martin Luther, *Tischreden aus den Jahren 1538–1540*, Weimar Ausgabe Tischreden 4 (Weimar: Böhlaus Nachfolger, 1916), no. 5223.
16. *LW* 44:66–68.
17. I'm indebted to my colleague Patrick Keifert for this insightful expression.
18. *LW* 12 (on Ps 19:10): "That is, the Gospel is kind, comforting, and sweet, for it rejoices consciences."
19. See Timothy Wengert, ed., *The Roots of Reform*, The Annotated Luther 1 (Minneapolis: Fortress, 2013), 167–255.
20. For a detailed study of Luther's rewriting of the sacraments, see Lange, *Trauma Recalled*.

21. Edward Yarnold, *Cyril of Jerusalem* (New York: Routledge, 2000), "Mystagogical Catechesis 2," 173–75.

22. Yarnold, *Cyril of Jerusalem*, 173–75.

23. See Daniel Stevick, "Types of Baptismal Spirituality," *Worship* 47 (1973): 11–26.

24. Luther, *Large Catechism*, 461.

25. Maxwell Johnson, *The Rites of Christian Initiation: Their Evolution and Interpretation* (Collegeville, MN: Liturgical Press, 2007), 317.

26. Luther, *Large Catechism*, 466.

27. Luther's attention to and use of metaphor is particularly noteworthy here. Luther engages a theological debate about baptism and penance by deconstructing the metaphor Jerome uses. He points out the trap of the metaphor—the ship breaks apart. Are we equally as attentive to the metaphors and illustrations we use in presiding and in preaching? Do the metaphors and illustrations convey the gospel message?

28. *LW* 36:74.

29. This realization puts into a new perspective many other vows we pronounce.

30. *LW* 35:32.

31. *Theologia Deutsch*, a work that significantly influenced Luther. See discussion in Chapter 6.

32. *LW* 35:33.

33. Mülhaupt, *Psalmen Auslegung*, 20.

34. Luther, *Small Catechism*, *BC* 360.

35. *LW* 36:258.

36. *LW* 35:38.

37. See Taylor, *Secular Age*.

38. Emmanuel Levinas, *Entre Nous: On Thinking of the Other*, trans. Michael B. Smith and Barbara Harshav (New York: Columbia University Press, 2000), 91–101.

39. *LW* 35:39.

40. See discussion of Bonhoeffer in Chapter 2.

CHAPTER 5: COMMUNAL PRAYER

1. Louis Martyn, *Theological Issues in the Letters of Paul* (Nashville: Abingdon, 1997), 87–88, 111–23.
2. See the Pentecost sequence from the Roman Catholic liturgy for Pentecost: "*Veni Sanct Spiritus*—Come, Holy Spirit, send forth the heavenly radiance of your light. . . . Bend that which is inflexible."
3. Luther compares the blessed to the trees planted by streams of water in his commentary on Ps 1:3: "They are like trees planted by streams of water, which yield their fruit in its season, and their leaves do not wither" (*WA* 5:36).
4. Mülhaupt, *Psalmen Auslegung*, 3–4.
5. Mülhaupt, *Psalmen Auslegung* , 4.
6. Mülhaupt, *Psalmen Auslegung*, 14.
7. Prayer of Peace, "Ecumenism and Righteousness" (November 14, 1988), in St. Nicholas Church, Leipzig.
8. *LW* 11 (on Ps 85:10).
9. Martin Luther, *Small Catechism*, in *BC* 352, 356.
10. Two eminent liturgical historians, Robert Taft, SJ, and Paul Bradshaw, have documented this diversity of practices and patterns.
11. "*Tout chrétien*," writes Max Thurian, "*par le baptême . . . exprime ainsi, dans sa prière, la louange des créatures.*" Thurian, *L'Office de Taizé*, 3rd ed. (Taizé: Les Presses de Taizé, 1964), vii. My translation: "Every Christian, through baptism, expresses in their prayer, the praise of all creation."
12. Paul Bradshaw, *Daily Prayer in the Early Church* (New York: Oxford University Press, 1982), 39.
13. Bradshaw, *Daily Prayer*, 39.
14. "*Le temps est un concept qui signifie que tout n'a pas été donné a la fois, mais qu'il y a creation de réalité nouvelle d'une maniere progressive et incessante, que le réel est en train de se faire, en train d'etre, petit a petit, inventé.*" Claude Tresmonant, *Essai sur la pensee hebraique* (Paris: Editions du Cerf, 1953), 26.
15. Bradshaw, *Daily Prayer*, 65.

16. Jean-Paul Sartre, *Qu'est-ce que la littérature?* (Paris: Gaillimard, 1948).
17. See J. Mateos, "The Origin of the Divine Office," *Worship* 41 (1967): 477–85; Mateos, "The Morning and Evening Office," *Worship* 42 (1968): 31–47; A. de Vogüé, *The Rule of Saint Benedict: A Doctrinal and Spiritual Commentary*, trans. J. B. Hasbrouck, Cistercian Studies 54 (Kalamazoo, MI: Cistercian Publications, 1983), 127–72.
18. John Cassian, *Institutions cénobitiques* (*De Institutis coenobiorum et de octo principalium vitiorum remediis*), ca. 420.
19. De Vogüé, *Rule of Saint Benedict*, 209.
20. De Vogüé, *Rule of Saint Benedict*, 209.
21. Bonhoeffer, *Prayerbook of the Bible*, 155.
22. Pierre Riché, *Césaire d'Arles*, (Paris: Les Éditions Ouvrières, 1958), *Sermon* 76.1.
23. Seigfried Raeder, *Grammatica Theologica: Studien zu Luthers Operationes in Psalmos* (Tübingen: Mohr Siebeck, 1977), 263 (*WA* 5:34).
24. Mülhaupt, *Psalmen Auslegung*, 3.
25. Raeder, *Grammatica Theologica*, 264. My translation. "When God reveals God's self in the word, the vocation or practice (exercise) of human beings is defined."
26. Raeder, *Grammatica Theologica*, 264.
27. Bonhoeffer, *Prayerbook of the Bible*, 155–56.
28. Bonhoeffer, *Prayerbook of the Bible*, 157.
29. *LW* 53:61.

CHAPTER 6: PATTERNS INTERRUPTED

1. Werner Leich (bishop), interview by author (July 15, 2010).
2. Reiner Kunze (1933–) is a German writer and former East German dissident. He resided in East Germany until expatriated in 1977.
3. Martin Henker (superintendent), interview by author (November 19, 2010).
4. Henker, interview.
5. Henker, interview.

6. Leich, interview.
7. Sievers, interview.
8. Mülhaupt, *Psalmen Auslegung*, 5.
9. Luther, "Treatise on Good Works," 64.
10. *WA* 5:239.
11. The version from which Luther worked remains unknown, though an original was found in Frankfurt, thus the German title "The Frankfurter." See Wolfgang von Hinten, *Der Franckforter (Theologia Deutsch), Kritische Textausgabe* (München: Artemis Verlag, 1982).
12. "*Vnde aller disser geteilten ist keynes das volkumen*" (von Hinten, *Der Franckforter*, 71).
13. Terence Fretheim, *God and the World in the Old Testament* (Nashville: Abingdon, 2005), 41, 62.
14. "*Wan kumpt ess [volkommende] aber? Ich sprech: Wanne ess, also verre als moglich ist, bekant, entpfunden vnnd gesmeckt wirt yn der sele*" (When does the perfect come? I say: When it is, as it is possible, recognized, sensed and tasted in the soul; von Hinten, *Der Franckforter*, 72).
15. Bonhoeffer: self-justification results in judgment.
16. Propst Heino Falcke, interview by author (November 18, 2010).
17. Grotowski, *Towards a Poor Theatre*, 17.
18. Pastor Wolfgang Groeger (see Chapter 2).
19. Jacques-Paul Migne, ed., *Patrologia Graeca* (Paris, 1862), 59:721–24.
20. See Shelly Rambo's significant work *Spirit and Trauma: A Theology of Remaining* (Louisville: Westminster John Knox, 2010) and *Resurrecting Wounds: Living in the Aftermath of Trauma* (Waco, TX: Baylor University Press, 2017).
21. *WA* 2:84.
22. *WA* 2:85. "*Darum soll man sich an die Worte halten und an denselben nach oben steigen, solange bis die Federn wachsen, dass man ohne Worte zu fliegen vermag.*" *LW* 42:25.
23. *WA* 2:85. *LW* 42:25.
24. *WA* 2:85. *LW* 42:25.
25. *WA* 2:84. *LW* 42:23–24.

26. *WA* 37:428–29. *"Darumb heisst er Gott loben inn der stille, das ist, das man nicht ungedultig werde, sondern lerne verzihen und harren und imer anhalte im glauben."*
27. *WA* 37:429.
28. For example, in French see André Chouraqui, trans., *La Bible* (Paris: Desclée de Brouwer, 1989). *"Pour toi, le silence est louange, Elohîm, en Siôn."*

POSTLUDE: PRAYER IN A TIME OF PHYSICAL DISTANCING

1. Prof. Dr. Joy Moore, Academic Dean, Luther Seminary, Sermon on Juneteenth (June 19, 2020).

BIBLIOGRAPHY

Bayer, Oswald. *Martin Luther's Theology: A Contemporary Interpretation*. Translated by Thomas H. Trapp. Grand Rapids: Eerdmans, 2008.

Becker, Ernest. *The Denial of Death*. New York: Free Press, 1997.

Bonhoeffer, Dietrich. *Discipleship*. Minneapolis: Fortress, 2003.

———. *Letters and Papers from Prison*. Minneapolis: Fortress, 2010.

———. *Life Together* and *Prayerbook of the Bible*. Minneapolis: Fortress, 2005.

Bradshaw, Paul F. *Daily Prayer in the Early Church*. New York: Oxford University Press, 1982.

Butler, Judith. *Gender Trouble: Feminism and the Subversion of Identity*. New York: Routledge, 2006.

Caruth, Cathy. *Trauma: Explorations in Memory*. Baltimore: Johns Hopkins University Press, 1995.

———. *Unclaimed Experience: Trauma, Narrative, and History*. Baltimore: Johns Hopkins University Press, 1996.

Certeau, Michel de. *The Capture of Speech and Other Political Writings*. Minneapolis: University of Minnesota Press, 1997.

———. *The Practice of Everyday Life*. Berkeley: University of California Press, 2011.

Fretheim, Terence. *God and the World in the Old Testament*. Nashville: Abingdon, 2005.

Jenson, Robert. "The Praying Animal." *Zygon* 18, no. 3 (September 1983): 311–25.

John Paul II. "Message of His Holiness Pope John Paul II for the XXIX World Day of Peace." Vatican, January 1, 1996. https://tinyurl.com/v6csl9j.

Johnson, Maxwell. *The Rites of Christian Initiation: Their Evolution and Interpretation*. Collegeville, MN: Liturgical Press, 2007.

Lathrop, Gordon W., and Timothy J. Wengert. *Christian Assembly: Marks of the Church in a Pluralistic Age*. Minneapolis: Fortress, 2004.

Levinas, Emmanuel. *Entre Nous: On Thinking of the Other*. Translated by Michael B. Smith and Barbara Harshav. New York: Columbia University Press, 2000.

Luther, Martin. "Disputation on Justification." *LW* 34:149–57.

———. *The Large Catechism*. *BC* 379–479.

———. "Meditation on the Passion of Christ." *LW* 42:7–14.

———. "On Rogationtide Prayer and Procession." *LW* 42:87–92.

———. "Preface to the Latin Works." *LW* 34:325–38.

———. *Small Catechism*. *BC* 347–71.

————. *Tischreden aus den Jahren 1538–1540*. Weimarer Ausgabe Tischreden 4. Weimar: Böhlaus Nachfolger, 1916.

————. "Treatise on Good Works." *LW* 44:17–114.

Lutheran World Federation. "The Church in the Public Space: A Study Document of the Lutheran World Federation." 2016. https://tinyurl.com/uvss5hj.

Martyn, Louis. *Theological Issues in the Letters of Paul*. Nashville: Abingdon, 1997.

Mateos, J. "The Morning and Evening Office." *Worship* 42 (1968): 31–47.

————. "The Origin of the Divine Office." *Worship* 41 (1967): 477–85.

O'Connor, Flannery. "Revelation." In *The Complete Short Stories*, 488–509. New York: Farrar, Straus, & Giroux, 1971.

Rambo, Shelly. *Resurrecting Wounds: Living in the Aftermath of Trauma*. Waco, TX: Baylor University Press, 2017.

————. *Spirit and Trauma: A Theology of Remaining*. Louisville: Westminster John Knox, 2010.

Rasmussen, Larry L. *Dieterich Bonhoeffer: Reality and Resistance*. Louisville: Westminster John Knox, 2005.

Saliers, Don E. *The Soul in Paraphrase: Prayer and the Religious Affections*. 5th ed. White Sulphur Springs, WV: OSL, 2015.

Soelle, Dorothee. *The Silent Cry: Mysticism and Resistance*. Minneapolis: Fortress, 2001.

Stolt, Birgit. *Martin Luther: Rhetorik des Herzen*. Stuttgart: Mohr Siebeck, 2000.

Taylor, Charles. *A Secular Age*. Cambridge, MA: Belknap Press of Harvard University Press, 2007.

Thompson, Deanne. *Crossing the Divide: Luther, Feminism and the Cross.* Minneapolis: Fortress, 2004.

Trelstad, Marit, ed. *Cross Examinations: Readings on the Meaning of the Cross Today.* Minneapolis: Fortress, 2006.

Vogüé, A. de. *The Rule of Saint Benedict: A Doctrinal and Spiritual Commentary.* Translated by J. B. Hasbrouck. Cistercian Studies 54. Kalamazoo, MI: Cistercian Publications, 1983.

Wengert, Timothy, ed. *The Roots of Reform.* The Annotated Luther 1. Minneapolis: Fortress, 2013.

ACKNOWLEDGMENTS

The heart of this book arises out of my experience of God's promise, known in community, through prayer, through word and sacrament, and in continual encounter with neighbors, both familiar and unfamiliar. In my introduction, I make a profound bow to those who served as my dialogue partners for this book: to the young people and pastors in former East Germany and to my mother, my first teacher of prayer. My formation in prayer happened also at the Community of Taizé (www.taize.fr), which has not only renewed and revived the practice of communal prayer in our day but has also forged a way toward reconciliation, within oneself, with God, between churches, and within the human family—and all this, through prayer.

There are also many other colleagues and friends who have come alongside me to make this book a reality. My faculty colleagues at Luther Seminary were constant, stimulating, and provocative dialogue partners years ago, as we worked on a major curricular revision resulting in a generative—dare I say confessional—statement that became the theological rationale for Luther Seminary's curriculum: God's unconditional promise creates and shapes who we are; community around word and sacrament embodies God's promises for us; the world of neighbors, both familiar and different, engages us in God's continually creative and good activity.

After the faculty adopted this new curriculum, I had the privilege to go on sabbatical, for which I thank the board of Luther Seminary and the two deans who watched over my academic formation: Roland Martinson and Craig Koester. If there is one place a faculty member can be creative, exploratory, and innovative, it is during this time of sabbatical, when space allows for new horizons to be imagined for both church and Christian presence in the world.

My sabbatical was also supported by a fellowship from the Herzog August Bibliothek (www.hab.de) in Wolfenbüttel, Germany. I am grateful to Dr. Timothy J. Wengert, teacher and colleague, for pointing me in the direction of the library, as well as Dr. Wesley Stevens, who has accompanied me since my college years and is still, in his nineties, working on a dictionary of medieval mathematical terminology. At that amazing international library, housing books spanning centuries of writing in all disciplines (beginning in the Middle Ages and early modern Europe to current scholarship), I was able to work on several translations of Luther's works; his sacramental treatises, treatises on prayer, and the German mass were my focus. I was able to work from first-edition print copies of these writings, a few of which had notations by Luther himself.

These translations have become part of Fortress Press's Annotated Luther Series (volumes 1 and 3 in particular). The original draft of this book was also written in those silent aulas, surrounded by many manuscripts and scholars from all over the globe with whom I could discuss theological, philosophical, and linguistic concepts, as well as translation conundrums. In particular, I valued the insights of Professor Robert Kolb. I am deeply grateful to the year spent at that Herzog August Library and for the now-retired director of the fellowship program, Dr. Jill Bepler. Her welcome, her suggestions, her guidance, and her friendship—not only to me but to my wife, Ilona, and children—were exemplary. The whole staff, under the direction of Frau Strauss, is especially to be thanked, for they embodied the welcome in many practical ways and helped make the sabbatical an enriching time for my whole family.

As the manuscript reached its final stages, the encouragement of Tim Blevins and Scott Tunseth was instrumental in keeping me on track. Beth Lewis had shared the manuscript with Tim, who was intrigued by a book that dived deeply into a Lutheran perspective on spirituality. Scott then had enough patience with me throughout the process—a process that saw me transition into different leadership and administrative positions at Luther Seminary, making research and scholarly work at times difficult. I'm indebted to Scott and also to Carol Throntveit for their meticulous and fine reading of the manuscript and all their great suggestions for improvement.

Throughout the process, friends came alongside me when the task of writing and publishing was not so easy, especially my colleagues Professor Matthew L. Skinner (New Testament), Professor Karoline M. Lewis (homiletics), and

Professor Guillermo Hansen (systematic theology). Their confidence in me kept me going.

Finally, but certainly not least, my dear wife, Ilona, deserves more thanks than I could give her, because she is incredibly patient with me and the time it takes to accomplish my work.

As I traveled around the globe lecturing on worship, Lutheran liturgy, the Lutheran confessions, and the Joint Commemoration of the Five Hundredth Anniversary of the Reformation celebrated in the Cathedral of Lund, Sweden, with Pope Francis, I developed and presented parts of this manuscript. Over and over, laypeople and pastors asked me: When will you publish these stories? I hope they all find what they were expecting in these pages. It is for them, for the church, for many communities of faith, for people searching what faith is and how faith engages us, that this book is also written.

Dirk G. Lange

Easter 2020—when everything was different

THEOLOGY FOR CHRISTIAN MINISTRY

Informing and inspiring Christian leaders and communities to proclaim God's *Word* to a *World* God created and loves. Articulating the fullness of both realities and the creative intersection between them.

Word & World Books is a partnership between Luther Seminary, the board of the periodical *Word & World*, and Fortress Press.

Books in the series include:

Rooted and Renewing: Imagining the Church's Future in Light of Its New Testament Origins by Troy M. Troftgruben (2019)

Journeying in the Wilderness: Forming Faith in the 21st Century by Terri Martinson Elton (2020)

God So Enters into Relationships That . . . : A Biblical View by Terence E. Fretheim (2020)

Today Everything Is Different: An Adventure in Prayer and Action by Dirk G. Lange (2021)